MW01277263

Rikhiapeeth Satsangs

With kind regards, ॐ *and prem*

Swami Niranjan

Rikhiapeeth Satsangs

Swami Satyananda Saraswati

*Satsangs given by Sri Swamiji at Rikhiapeeth, Deoghar,
during the period 2000–2007*

Yoga Publications Trust, Munger, Bihar, India

© Sivananda Math 2007

All rights reserved. No part of this publication may be reproduced, transmitted or stored in a retrieval system, in any form or by any means, without permission in writing from Yoga Publications Trust.

The terms Satyananda Yoga® and Bihar Yoga® are registered trademarks owned by International Yoga Fellowship Movement (IYFM). The use of the same in this book is with permission and should not in any way be taken as affecting the validity of the marks.

Published by Yoga Publications Trust
First edition 2007

ISBN: 978-81-86336-66-3

Publisher and distributor: Yoga Publications Trust, Ganga Darshan, Munger, Bihar, India.

Website: www.biharyoga.net

Printed at Thomson Press (India) Limited, New Delhi, 110001

Dedication

*In humility we offer this dedication to
Swami Sivananda Saraswati, who initiated
Swami Satyananda Saraswati into the secrets of yoga.*

Contents

INTELLECT AND INTUITION

Source of inspiration

How do we find and maintain inspiration? Inspiration can be direct and inspiration can also be had through the intellect. After all, you want inspiration, and you are thinking through the intellect. Just like blood flows through the arteries, but can also flow through collateral veins, we can have inspiration directly without any involvement of the intellect and also through the intellect. The intellect does understand.

Practically speaking, there is not a big difference between the intellect and intuition, reasoning and experience. When I read the *Bhagavad Gita*, I place myself in the situation of Arjuna and place my higher self in the place of Krishna, and change the scene of the battlefield. It becomes the scene of my life: my family, office, shop, industry, wife, children, court case, politics. For me, the enemies that have to be subdued are not outside of me. So I am using and involving the intellect to find inspiration. The army I want to subdue does not consist of human beings; it consists of my instincts. I am the warrior. I am the commander-in-chief, Arjuna, and my higher self is Krishna. Now the question comes: is this way of thinking, which is intellectual, sufficient to progress in spiritual life?

1

Transcending intellect

We do not need to transform the intellect, as some people believe, but there comes a time when we need to transcend it. It is somewhat like this. You go from Rikhia to Delhi by train; your vehicle is the train. But you cannot use a train to go from Delhi to Greece. You have to leave the train behind and now go by air. So there is a time in life when the intellect is a helper and there is a time when you have to transcend the intellect because it cannot go beyond a certain point. Intellect can go a very great distance. It can probe into anything without having had a direct experience. It can probe into God, into mysterious experiences, into the past, going back to millions of years. However, there is a limit to intellect, and there comes a point when you have to transcend it.

So, to expect that you will get inspiration intuitionally right now is not proper, because there is no airport at Rikhia! You have to take the train. You cannot handle intuition because you do not have intuition right now. Go through the intellect and after some time, when it is the right time, you will transcend it naturally. You will not have to think about it.

The meeting point

The West is primarily intellectual. There everything is tested through the intellect. But then what happens? The intellect probes into subjects, an objective perception is taken, and finally it comes round to the same point where intuition arrives.

It was with the help of the intellect that Darwin formed his theory of evolution. It was also said that earth will come to an end in 5000 years, but now nobody believes that. Now, another theory has been postulated, that life on earth came from some other planet during a meteoric explosion. Through genetic research it was found that the gene is older than the age of the earth. The earth is four and a half billion years old, but life is five billion years old. So it must have come from outside. All this was discovered through the intellect. The West proceeds through intellectual probing into a subject,

2

going further and further, and arrives at the same point where you can arrive through intuition. There is a point where intellectual and intuitional achievements meet. You must have faith in the intellect. People think that intellect is inferior; I have heard this particularly from Westerners, who think that the intellect is materialistic. No, the intellect is an instrument that can help you probe into things, and which you have at your beck and call. Intuition is not at the beck and call of the ordinary person. Everybody cannot handle intuition because they cannot have it. Only a few people such as Christ, Buddha or Shankaracharya had access to intuition. Everyone, however, possesses intellect. It is an instrument that you have at hand to probe with.

You must also remember that *jnana yoga* is the yoga of intellect. Even Shankaracharya said that through the intellect you can go very far, even transcend the material perception. If the intellect becomes purified through spiritual processes, you can stay with intuition, there is no difference between intellect and intuition. Purified intellect is intuition. It is the same energy.

BE RESPONSIBLE FOR YOURSELF

Every individual is responsible for himself, and we should all realize this. No one can change another person. This is a conclusion that I have come to. Every person is responsible for changing his own good or bad traits. I am the one who can correct myself; you cannot do it and the police cannot do it. All the sages have said that whatever is within you, whether joy, sorrow, alcoholism or any other bad habit, it is not possible for someone else to remove it from your life.

You should accept the good qualities through your own convictions and eliminate the undesirable qualities through your own convictions also. If you are convinced that you are right, then do it. And if you are convinced that you are wrong, give it up. I used to teach all over the world and when people would ask me if they should give up alcohol, I would reply, "If you want to drink, drink. I do not hold judgement on this." However, if you want to get rid of a negative trait, do not become obsessed with it; be indifferent to it. The more obsessive you are, the more strongly it will hold you in its clutches.

Hatha yoga is a solution to get rid of all impurities. It includes asana, pranayama, mudra and bandha. Do three or four asanas and one or two pranayamas every day. There are only three kinds of pranayama – inhalation, exhalation and retention. These three are modified in different ways in different practices. There are many mudras, pick two or three that you prefer. *Bandha* means to bind, to bind mooladhara, vishuddhi or manipura. So, practise asana, pranayama, mudra and bandha for half an hour or forty-five minutes, no more. Do not practise for two or three hours. And do not think that you are practising to get rid of your alcoholism. To give up alcohol is not the aim of your life. The aim of life is not to struggle to give up vices, because there is nothing called 'vice'. A vice is a shadow, just as a tree has a shadow. To remove the shadow, you will have to cut down the tree. There is not one negative quality that exists within you, there are many. They are all shadows, *maya*, unreal.

GURU-DISCIPLE RELATIONSHIP

What is a true guru-disciple relationship? Nowadays many gurus cheat their disciples.
The guru-disciple relationship is a vast matter. We have had this tradition from ancient times. There are different kinds of gurus – the *kula guru* is the family guru and there is the *adhyatmic* or spiritual guru. A relationship does exist between the guru and disciple, but it is not necessary that it is maintained consistently by everyone. The guru-disciple relationship is a very high realization. It is very difficult to explain. Do not expect that you will instantly have a hotline, telepathic connection, with the guru.

Receiving sadhana
The guru-disciple relationship is necessary because a guru is necessary for spiritual growth. All religions, philosophies, sages and seers have said in one voice that it is necessary to take guru mantra. The relationship starts with the mantra; it is the main basis of the guru-disciple relationship. The beginning is the mantra and later, when the guru feels that the disciple is making progress, other sadhanas are given. After all, not all sadhanas can be given right at the beginning. The guru will not give you all the lessons at one go. You have to start from A, B, C, D. First do your japa, and after a year or two years he will tell you to do something else. If you are a singer, he may ask you to chant Om every morning. He may ask you to do bhramari at four in the morning because he can see that you are inclined that way. Or, if he finds that your mind is very restless – you go to sleep at one a.m., wake up at two p.m., travel around the world, deal with taxes – he may ask you to do some pranayama in the morning so that your nervous system is not adversely affected. If you are trying to overcome a big obstacle, he may ask you to perform an anushthana. In this way, by handling the disciple slowly, the guru brings him to such a state that the disciple realizes

that whatever is happening in his life, whatever will happen or has happened, was fixed. You acquire the knowledge of karma and of the one who makes karma; you acquire the knowledge of destiny.

Basis of guru

Many people search for gurus. What is the basis of a guru? On what basis do you make a guru? Just as there has to be a basis for finding a husband or wife, there has to be some basis for finding a guru. The basis has to be something that keeps the relationship stable. The guru-disciple relationship should be consistent and eternal. Many people go on searching for a guru and go on measuring him with a measuring tape. "He is not five inches and seven centimetres long. Cancel!"

The relationship between a guru and disciple is the same as that between a boy and a girl. One look and you have fallen in love! Bhakti has awakened. The mind has become completely quiet. You should not have any parameters to judge the guru with. When you have just entered a school, you do not ask the qualifications of the master. You are a fool, so how will you understand his qualifications? You are trying to investigate whether or not the guru is good enough for you when you do not have the capability to do so! Go to the guru with an empty mind, search for a guru with an empty mind. The relationship between the guru and disciple is such that when you go to the guru, the mind becomes quiet.

When I left home, I went to Rajasthan. I had an adopted sister there who was a doctor. She was interested in spiritual things so I thought she might be able to tell me something. She gave me the address of her guru. I went there, and he was very happy to see me as he thought that an educated boy like me could look after the ashram for him. He saw me as a prospective successor. He was a good man. I learnt a lot from him. He was very knowledgeable on the theoretical aspects of tantra. I stayed there for six months. I had great respect for him and he, too, held me in respect. But one day,

6

something happened in my head. I said to myself, "I do not want to become a successor. If I have to look after property, I might as well go back home." So I scaled the twelve-foot-high wall of the ashram and ran away.

I took a train in which I met a mahatma with matted hair and a long beard. He asked, "Where are you going?" I replied, "I want to become a disciple, I need a guru." He became furious and gave me a good scolding, but then he took me to Kali Kamliwala Gurudwara in Rishikesh, and said, "Search here, this is the place of gurus." The next day I went to Vishnudevanandaji at Kailash Ashram. I prostrated at his feet and said "I want to take sannyasa." He said, "Take sannyasa and come here, I will let you stay. But I will not give you sannyasa because I do not give sannyasa. I am only the acharaya of an akhara." Then he told me of Swami Sivananda.

The moment I saw Swami Sivananda, all my thoughts of searching for a guru ended. I said to myself, "Stay here." The person at whose very sight the desire for love ends and *shraddha*, faith, finds its fulfilment, is your guru. He is your lover. From then on, I stayed there.

The circumstances were very difficult. Our guru was not rich, we had to beg for food and sleep on the floor. We were bitten by mosquitoes, scorpions would crawl over us, there were snakes, and the water of the Ganga was dirty. But we were not bothered. When I remember those days I feel surprised at how I stayed there. Guruji would remain closed up in his room, and we would never get to meet him. He would remain in his kutir and we would be working outside. Now you may say that if the guru and disciple do not even meet, then how will the disciple learn?

I would cook food, clean utensils, bring water from the Ganga, chop wood, climb six kilometres uphill to the District Collector's office to get a permit to buy sugar from the ration shop. I did all that a servant does at home. I worked as a servant in the ashram. But those were such happy days! Sometimes I wish that I could leave this body and again live in an ashram like that because it is very nice to live as a disciple in an ashram;

it is no good living as a guru. The joy that exists in living as a disciple does not exist in living as a guru.

The guru-disciple relationship is in a way a relationship of love. The only difference is, whereas in the material world the basis of love is human life, here the basis of love is spiritual life. There you call it love; here you call it bhakti. There you call it *ishk majaji*; here you call it *ishk hakiki*. There you call it worldly love; here you call it spiritual love. Here two souls unite; and through such spiritual union the child of wisdom is born. After all, our Guruji made us give birth to children, did he not? But who is the child that we gave birth to? The form of that child is *jnana*, wisdom.

It is essential to have a guru. Whether you want to study till the primary or mid level, in college or university, you need a teacher. In the same way, if you want to know how to walk the spiritual path, find a guru. Even if you just want to do mantra japa, find a guru. If you want to learn hatha yoga, raja yoga, bhakti yoga or jnana yoga, you will have to find a guru.

False gurus

Always remember this, even if a guru is not genuine, one day he will have to become genuine. Imagine for a moment that someone has put on the robes of a guru to cheat disciples. Even if that were so, he will not be able to continue this for very long. Sooner or later his spirit will awaken from within and force him to become a true guru. I have seen this happen to many people. I am not speaking of one or two false gurus who may exist. But there is no dearth of true gurus in this country.

India is the land of gurus. People come here in their thousands looking for gurus. Does anyone go to Russia to look for a guru? Do they go to America? They may go to America to study and earn money, but have you ever heard that someone is going to America to look for a guru? Anyone who wants to find a guru will have to come to India. This means that the whole world admits that gurus do exist in India. If you wish to challenge this, do so. The whole world from Alaska to the Falkland Islands to Ireland accepts that India is the land of gurus. This is where people can receive spiritual training. All western countries have yoga centres and spiritual centres in every nook and corner, but they still come to India to look for gurus. Why? Because just as a man and a woman's lives are incomplete without each other, an aspirant's spiritual life is also meaningless without a guru.

SANNYASA IN A MODERN WORLD

The sannyasa revolution
The idea of sannyasa is finding a good stronghold in the modern era. The number of people who have become sannyasins in the last ten to fifteen years is much more than in the past. Earlier, people would take sannyasa after the age of sixty when they believed that their desires had finished like a wrung-out cloth. But now those in the age group of eighteen to thirty come for sannyasa, and in large numbers. There is a large number in America, Australia and Europe, and they wear geru and shave their heads.

This century is going to be very different from the centuries that have gone by. This is a century of revolution. There may come a time when children will not have to go to school; they will be able to do all their studies at home. People will not have to go to the office or the bank; everything will be accomplished at home through computers. This is already happening in the world. You order things on the telephone, you exchange news on the telephone; there is no need to visit personally any more. You cook food in three minutes in the microwave. However, all these things will have their effect on the mind.

With so much time to spare, what will you do? This is a point worth thinking about. An idle mind is the devil's workshop. I spotted this problem in Europe in 1968. I said to myself, "These people have only one problem. They do not have any work." The empty mind, which is going to be a syndrome of this century, has only one solution. It can only be filled up through one thing, the search for God. Every ounce of energy is used up in the search for God. In this century not much effort will be required to earn money. So the mind can be occupied with God-realization.

Take the train

People ask me if they should take sannyasa. I say, "Yes, do." Then they say, "What if the mind fluctuates afterwards." I say, "Let it fluctuate, it does not matter." If you think, "What if the boat overturns!" before even sitting in a boat and therefore do not take the boat, that's not the right thing to do. Accidents do happen, but people still use aeroplanes. If an accident happens in sannyasa, let it happen. Accidents are part of this world. However, not all sannyasins have accidents, only a few do. You hear about them and get scared. Accidents happen, but people do not lose heart due to them; they still take the train.

Some people prefer to take karma sannyasa. The *Bhagavad Gita* describes the idea – even while living in the world and being immersed in everyday tasks, a karma sannyasin still binds himself to the rules of sannyasa. It is very good to bind yourself

10

to the rules of sannyasa. When you come to the ashram, wear geru and shave your head; when you are at home, wear whatever you like. Hair grows back in a few days anyway.

Become a witness
The easiest way to self-realization is to look at the whole world in the same way as you look at the stage in a theatre or film. The outlook is that of a witness, *sakshi*. Whatever is happening in your life, keep watching it. You are the observer, you are not the actor. Watch the pleasure, watch the pain, watch whatever happens. Watch yourself completely, whether you are drinking alcohol, performing worship, getting angry or conducting business. You are the *jivatma*, the individual soul, who is the actor. *Paramatma*, the supreme soul, is the *drashta*, the seer. The seer watches the actor.

EXPERIENCING YOURSELF

When the fluctuations of the mind cease and the mental faculty comes back to its even level, just like the ocean comes to its even level when the tide has ebbed, the state is called *sambuddhi*, even-mindedness. Sambuddhi is samadhi. When the intellect is freed of its state of fluctuation, it is called *samadhi*. The sign of samadhi is that the mind gives up its state of fluctuation, it stops moving, and experiences an effulgent being within itself; it experiences itself. *Swaroope avasthanam* – it becomes established in its own identity.

For example, there is a mad man and he calls himself Hitler. When the doctor gives him an injection, his mind comes back to its normal state and he is again established in his own identity. In the same way, we call ourselves brahmin, shudra, male, female, rich, poor, big, small, Hindu and Muslim, but these are not our real identities. Our real identity is the atman. Even though the atman does not have any special form, we can say that the most beautiful form of the atman is *shanti*, peace. Its real form is shanti, a state where there is no noise within or without.

Samadhi is a subject of raja yoga. It has been divided into three categories: savikalpa, nirvikalpa and nirbija. Savikalpa samadhi has been further divided into four categories: tarka, vitarka, asmita and ananda. Read my book *Four Chapters on Freedom*, where all this has been described in detail: what is samadhi, how do you experience asmita and ananda, is a person awake or asleep in these states, and so on.

Atma darshan

Tulsidas had the experience of Hanuman, Guru Ramdas had the darshan of Hanuman and Moses witnessed a burning bush. What is all this? This experience, where nothing visible exists, but you still see something – what is that? If that which is not there is experienced, it is a result of samadhi. This is *savikalpa samadhi*.

The sages have two definitions of the relationship between the jivatma and paramatma: there is a difference between the two, and there is no difference. There is no difference between me and the supreme soul means whatever I am, you are. Whatever you are, I am. I am not me and you are not you. This is called *abheda*, undivided. *Jivobrahma eva* – "The jivatma is like the Brahman." There is no difference, just as there is no difference between the bangle on your wrist and the gold it is made from. They are not two separate things, yet they are separate, too. The form is the bangle and the basis is gold. So there is no difference, and there is a difference as well.

When in savikalpa samadhi you have the vision of something, you see it as different from you. But the difference is only being experienced by you; in fact, there is no difference. The experience is taking place within you, but you feel as if you are seeing it outside yourself in the same way that you think you see a ghost outside of you when it is within you. Savikalpa samadhi is a certain kind of experience, in which the devotee sees God as separate from himself. The jivatma experiences the dual, *dwaita*, nature of paramatma. He sees God in different forms. He does not experience God in the form of Soham. His experience is not that of Soham Shivoham

12

Satchidananda Swaroopoham. He feels that he and param-atma are different. This experience of the difference occurs in savikalpa samadhi, in bhakti.

In raja yoga it is said that when savikalpa samadhi occurs, the aspirant experiences his atman as an objective experience. Someone experiences it as *jyoti*, light, someone as *nada*, subtle sound, and someone else as *shruti*, hearing of sacred words. The sages experienced their atman in the form of shruti and wrote the Vedas – therefore, the Vedas are also called shrutis. Mohammed also experienced shruti; he heard the whole of the *Koran*, and Moses experienced it in a burning bush.

Purity of mind

Different saints and sages have described their experience of the atman in different ways. Sri Aurobindo wrote of his experience in the Alipore Jail. Ramakrishna Paramahamsa experienced Mother Kali. All these sages had reached a very high state. Their mind had become pure. Ramakrishna Paramahamsa's mind had become so pure that he saw the Mother in his own wife. It is very hard to see the mother principle in your wife. Ramakrishna Paramahamsa reached this state because his mental state had become pure, it was without modifications. In this state he had the vision of Kali, and he saw Kali just as you would see another person. It was no illusion for him, it was no experience; it was darshan. If you come to my house or I go to your house, will you call it an internal experience or an actual meeting? So he actually met her. Many similar incidents are related from the lives of Adi Shankaracharya, Surdas, Mirabai, and others.

What an innocent life Mirabai had! She was not a mad woman. How did a girl of six or fourteen accept a statue of Krishna as her husband? Do you ever think about this? I think about it. Agreed that a girl of six is very innocent and if you tell her, "This is your husband", she will accept it. But when she grows up and it is time for her to get married, will she accept that a statue is her husband? Mira did. There can be only two meanings of this: either she was mad or she had reached such a high spiritual state that she could realize the vision, the reality, the depth of Krishna within that statue.

If you give a piece of gold to an ordinary person, he will think it is brass, but if you give it to a goldsmith, he will say that it is gold because he has realized the gold in it. In the same way, Mirabai realized that it was not a wooden statue, but Krishna, Giridhara, Kanhaiya himself. She experienced this. When her heart became so pure she experienced God, she had the darshan of God. And Mirabai did not die; she became one with light. Light became one with light; she did not leave her body behind anywhere. In the same way, Kabir did not leave behind a body when he died. When they lifted his shroud, they only found flowers. He too dissolved his body into light. All these things point to a high state and purity of mind. There is a state where the mind is not pure and there is a state where the mind is pure.

Pure and impure minds are two states of existence. We all know which of the two states we are in. If our mind is restless, we will perceive everything as broken, misshapen, untidy and dilapidated. If our mind is pure, we will perceive everything as whole. So to experience God within yourself, the first requirement is to make your mind pure.

SAT CHANDI MAHA YAJNA

I enjoy being with you. I don't try to avoid you or make myself unavailable. My anushthana ends every year on the Ekadashi of Kartik, in October–November. But this year I could not finish my prescribed practices because of many pilgrimages. I went to Badrinath, and also visited the ashram of my Guruji in Rishikesh twice. I went there for worship and conducted pooja, then visited many other places, including Vaishnav Devi near Jammu, which is a very important shrine of the Vaishnava sect. The comparable shrine of the Shakta sect is Kamakhya in Guwahati, Assam, which is considered to be the supreme seat of Shakti. Going to this place and that place, there was a gap in my sadhana of about thirty-five days. I could complete all the practices only yesterday morning, and so today I am here. So I don't try to avoid people; I live with the people, and I don't apologize for my absence.

15

108 KUMARIS

People often ask why the number 108 is auspicious. Actually, it is not 108; it is one – cipher – eight. One represents *Purusha*; eight represents *Prakriti*, the eightfold nature, and cipher represents blank, void or *shoonya*. When Purusha and Prakriti come together, there is creation. Eight plus one is nine. Now, if you take all the multiples of nine: $9 \times 2 = 18$, $9 \times 3 = 27$, $9 \times 4 = 36$, $9 \times 5 = 45$, each total is nine! All the multiplications of nine are nine and it never changes. Whether duality or destruction is there, the universe, the creation, continues. But remember there is no beginning and no end to this creation. There will not be a day when there is no creation. It was, it is and it will be. So it is exactly 108.

One represents Purusha and eight Prakriti, but to separate Prakriti from Purusha, you bring in the situation of vacuum, shoonya, non-existence, no mind. That is yoga. The number 108 represents the process of yoga, separation of Purusha from Prakriti by creating a state of vacuum, which is called *samadhi*. The cipher means zero, and zero means there is nothing. When the mind becomes quiet, there are no ripples. The state of shoonya arises when the mind is totally devoid of every experience: conscious, subconscious and unconscious. So, shoonya separates Purusha from Prakriti, samadhi separates Purusha from Prakriti, and that is the significance of one – zero – eight.

One hundred and eight girls will be worshipped in the Kumari Poojan, which will be performed here today. One hundred and eight represents the separation of Purusha and Prakriti. These children are mostly from our locality, but one is from France, one from New Zealand and one from the USA. Two of these are the children of sannyasins. Of course, I don't ask sannyasins to produce children because the population is already up to five or six billion. If all the sannyasins in India and the monks and nuns in the West were to start producing, the population would be up to seven billion in no time. Sannyasins are the family planning officers.

We do not need sannyasa in order to realize God, because God can be realized anywhere, but sannyasa is necessary in order to create balance and control in the world. At the same time, if a sannyasin should reproduce, the quality of this child will be better. I am not encouraging the sannyasins to have children, rather I would say, please don't do it. The quality of progeny is influenced by changes in the DNA, as a result of the thinking and living patterns of man. You can also alter your DNA by changing your lifestyle and way of thinking. These genetic changes take place through sannyasa. A sannyasin is a genetic engineer. He changes his prarabdha and his entire genetic personality. All the sannyasins are undergoing a process of genetic alteration. If you don't know about this, you can study genetic science.

What is DNA? How does it change? How does it evolve? How does it permute and combine? So these two children are born of sannyasins. I hope they will become sannyasins again.

AGRICULTURAL SOCIETY

We are starting an agricultural movement here in Rikhia. The best form of society is a prosperous agricultural society. This is a very sustainable society whereas an industrial society is not. In the long term, industrial fallout will be very harmful to the environment and to the health of the people. Of course, we cannot change this situation, but we can definitely express our opinion. I always feel that agriculture must be given prime importance throughout the world. Governments should concentrate on agriculture and promote an agricultural rural society. Rural society is a very important section of our world which all the nations worldwide have neglected.

An agricultural program called Sivananda Sarovar has developed behind this ashram on land donated by the local people. We have already planted medicinal herbs for ordinary illnesses. Strong medicines, like antibiotics, are generally not needed here, except for emergencies. There are plenty of herbs for most of the common illnesses, like coughs and

17

colds, stomach aches, itching and weakness. Many remedies can be prepared from ginger, onion, garlic and different types of leaves. The plants, leaves, bark, roots, flowers and fruits all have great medicinal value. Since all of us are now dependent on readymade medicines, we have forgotten practically everything about home remedies. We can't even identify the most common medicinal plants. There may be plants growing in our own garden or in the garden next door which can be used as medicine for our illnesses, but we don't even know about them.

So, agriculture is a versatile culture because it provides food as well as medicines. We must encourage the rural people to revive their herbal knowledge because they can grow medicinal herbs and sell them to make money. Many people have sent us seeds from all parts of the world: Australia, Greece and America also. Sometimes they send seeds of exotic flowers which don't have any market locally. Vegetables are marketable here and we can grow every kind of vegetable. We gave some of our exotic plants grown with foreign seeds to the agricultural college nearby. We supplied them with French mango, and now a new variety of mango has emerged. We created a small nursery here and supplied thirty to forty thousand trees to the local people, such as bamboo and rosewood. We also supply organic seeds to the local farmers, which can grow with natural fertilizers, so that they don't need to use chemical pesticides.

COSMIC MOTHER

Today is the last day of the Sat Chandi Yajna, which is performed to invoke the blessings and auspiciousness of the Mother. Soon the pandits will be lighting the ceremonial fire, which will bring our worship to a close. Although most of us are patriarchal, the Cosmic Mother is matriarchal. Mother is the first and God came next. This is what has been written in the *Devi Bhagavat Purana*, one of the epics of Shakti, in the form of Devi Bhagavat. Adi Shakti is the original or primal mother, who was not born from a womb. We are worshipping that eternal mother who has no particular form but every form is her form, even as gold has no particular form, silver has no particular form, earth has no particular form, water has no particular form and air has no particular form, but every form is their form. Every ornament is the form of gold; every pot is the form of clay. This is enough for us to understand that the mother has no particular form, which means every form is her form. We should not say that she is formless. She has no particular form, even as clay has no particular form, but every pot is a form of clay. It is her glory we see in the sun and moon, in all forms of life.

So, we are worshipping that Mother, whom yogis know as kundalini shakti, Vaishnavas as Lakshmi, Shaivas as Gauri and Amba, Christians as Mary, and today is the happy culmination of her worship. Mother is the giver and nourisher of life. At the same time, she has the power to bless everyone but she does not punish anyone. God may punish, because the father is known to get angry, but the mother is full of compassion and forgiveness. She has infinite tolerance. The children may go wrong, even the husband may go wrong, but mother never goes wrong. The son may turn out to be a bad son, but the mother never turns out to be a bad mother. This is the teaching of Shakta Tantra. Mother never punishes and, even if she gives a slap, she doesn't slap out of anger, she slaps out of love.

ANNA DAANAM

The fire ceremony which the pandits are conducting marks the successful culmination of this yajna. This year the prasad of the yajna was *patra*, utensils and containers. People came from all over the world and brought different kinds of containers. Now, the local people have all the vessels and containers they need in their kitchens. They have received such an abundance of containers over the last few days that they find their kitchens too small to contain them all. Next

19

year the prasad will be anna daanam, whether it is wheat, rice, maize or any other type of grain. By *anna*, food grains, we live. So, all the local people as well as the participants of the yajna will receive grains in abundance next year, as the prasad of the yajna.

I expect to receive grain from everyone next year, not flowers, not chocolates, not greeting cards. Our ancestors spoke of five grains: wheat, rice, gram, maize and mustard. These are the five foods which are most important for the survival of human beings. Flowers and greeting cards do not feed the hungry stomach. Everywhere, in every corner of the world, there are hungry souls whose children sleep without a morsel of food. Hunger and starvation exist not only in India but throughout the world. There are people who need food for survival in Africa, Asia, South America and even Europe and North America. Therefore, I say, "Feed man and God will be fed." If man dies hungry, God will also die. Because the existence of God depends on man.

I have lived amongst the poor all my life and my habits are like any poor man in India. Even if I wanted to live like the rich, I could not because I have lived with the poor and developed their habits. You may not have seen or heard about the poor, but I have seen and I have lived with them. Even now I live amongst them, they are all around me. So this is a very important injunction to every spiritual aspirant and to all of you. Next year do not bring candles. Candles are good inside churches and temples. Flowers are good when you want to meet your boyfriend or girlfriend. Greeting cards are good when you want to do business. But grain is necessary to feed the hungry stomach and, at the same time, it is necessary to maintain the law and order of the universe, *annad bhavanti bhutani*. This important truth is conveyed in the *Taittiriya Upanishad* and in the *Bhagavad Gita* as well.

CULTURAL REVIVAL

The ritual of yajna or sacrifice being performed here today was not accepted by Lord Buddha. His rejection of this practice was such an important platform of his teaching that it nearly became a movement in itself. Although yajna was sanctioned by the Vedas and considered to be a very great practice, Buddha refused to accept it because he was moved by the slaughter of animals, which was included in the yajnas of those times. He criticized this vedic ritual, because he was moved by compassion for the beings that were sacrificed.

From that time, in India the practice of sacrifice became almost extinct, although in the Vedas it is still upheld. So, in order to perform the yajna without offending this sentiment, what we do is improvise by replacing the animal with a cucumber. In Kamakhya, however, animal sacrifice is still permitted. Kamakhya is the *yoni peetha*, or the womb of the Mother, which is the most important peetha of Shakti. It is only there that real sacrifice, according to tantra, can still be conducted. Therefore, if a sacrifice is performed for any purpose, it is necessary to go to Kamakhya to fulfil that aspect of it; that can't be done here. The shakti peetha here in Deoghar is the *hridaya peetha*, which is the heart of the Mother. There are certain rituals in tantra, which can't be done here; they can only be done in Kamakhya.

Now the yajna has come to a close and the pandits who have performed it are chanting from the *Sama Veda*. Previously they were chanting from *Yajur Veda*. The *Rig Veda* is the most ancient Veda. According to Indian tradition, the *Sama Veda* is the root of all music. The notes of the seven octave scale: sa, re, ga, ma, pa, dha, ni, sa, emanate from the *Sama Veda*, which means the Veda of music. Next is the chanting from *Atharva Veda*, the fourth Veda, which contains the science of music, the science of medicine, the science of archery, the science of martial arts – all the sciences are found in this Veda. The chanting which you have heard must have been sung by our ancestors, thousands and thousands of years ago, but we still remember it today because we believe in inheritance.

In modern times, the two greatest needs of humanity are yoga for mental peace and yajna for prosperity. These two things are difficult to attain during the *Kali Yuga*, the age which we are in now. Yoga brings about a confluence of all the four *purusharthas* (human efforts): *artha* (financial stability), *kama* (emotional fulfilment), *dharma* (right living) and *moksha* (liberation). For this reason, everybody needs yoga today, even those who are very rich and powerful.

Everybody needs mental peace, *shanti*, and everybody needs prosperity, *samriddhi*. For obtaining these two needs, yajna is the vehicle. As long as the culture of yajna was prevalent, India was the Golden Bird. It is written in the annals of history, by people who came here from other parts of the world that India was a land of riches and prosperity. Today, of course, the picture is very different. The culture of yoga and yajna will have to be revived and propagated again, and then conditions will improve. These are the twin cultures of this land, both are very powerful and beneficial for each and every human being.

MARRIAGE OF SITA AND RAMA

So today, about 1.7 million years ago, at the end of *Treta Yuga*, the second era, Rama and Sita were married at Janakpuri, in the north of Bihar. Their marriage is described in the *Ramacharitamanas*. Rama was a very strong boy, dark in colour, like a black cloud. You can see that colouring in some of the local people sitting here today. Rama was *shyama*, dark in colour, and Sita was pure white. So we always sing the song: Sita Rama manohar jori; Dasharatha nandana janaka kishori. The celebration of the union of Sita and Rama represents the highest culmination of human ideals, which is not limited to any one culture, religion or race. I don't believe that Rama was Hindu, Buddha was Buddhist, or

22

Christ was Christian. Everyone knows that Christ was born a Jew and died a Jew.

Sita and Rama were married on this day seventeen lakh years ago. Not today, the 9th December, but the fifth day of the full moon of the month of Marga Sheersha. We are also celebrating that marriage symbolically today. I give the figure seventeen lakh years ago because a bridge has recently been discovered by an American satellite between Rameshwaram and Sri Lanka, and they have said that it is seventeen lakh years old. That is the same bridge, which the monkeys constructed for Sri Rama and his army to cross over to Sri Lanka. That bridge still remains underneath the water and a satellite has taken a picture of it. This is a very authentic statement, not a myth or an epic. It is a part of the history which you have forgotten, history beyond history.

TAPOVAN SANGEET

A new CD of my chanting called *Tapovan Sangeet* has come out. I will tell you the story of how those chants came to be recorded. Many years ago, I went to France and stayed with a homeopathic doctor, then I went to stay with Swami Devatmananda because there was no ashram at that time. She brought a small piano which I had to pump with my feet, like a Singer sewing machine, and then play. She recorded everything that I chanted, even the different Shanti Paths and many Hindi bhajans. Afterwards, she gave these recordings to a company, and they put them through a sound processor and made a long-playing record album from them. This was the only chanting tape that I ever made, although I can sing well. I could have made another album, but I said 'no' because I am a one-track person, master of one, not jack of all. So this is how *Tapovan Sangeet* was made. I have one condition, however, that this CD will be distributed free of charge and not sold commercially.

23

SAT CHANDI MAHA YAJNA

This year the Sat Chandi Maha Yajna has taken a different form. You are not my guests, nor the guests of Swami Niranjan or Swami Satsangi. This year, you are the guests of the Divine Mother's most beautiful form – the kanyas. The kanyas will welcome you when the rituals start tomorrow. I have only come here today to explain a little about the yajna, so that you can gain the maximum spiritual benefit from it.

Kanya means virgin. Man's soul is virgin. That virginity cannot be contaminated. Its pristine beauty and glory cannot be sullied. But you can't see that virgin soul; you don't know what it is or where it is in you. That purity of soul is the kanya, which is the next form of the Mother. This year, you will be the guests of that virgin soul, of that virgin reality who you don't know, who nobody knows. When you don't know an object, then you have to form a concept. This time, the concept is the kanyas of Rikhia who are sitting here. They are innocent and pure, and they represent your virgin soul, they represent your pure spirit, they represent your inner being, which you cannot and will not see.

24

In Devi tantra, the tantric system of the Cosmic Mother, the virgin is considered to be the true replica of the Cosmic Mother. From tomorrow, when the Sat Chandi Maha Yajna begins, you are not the master here, you are only servants. We are all servants of the Cosmic Mother. We are not her husband or her father. We are her children and she is our master. We should remember this and feel this. Neither you nor Swami Niranjan, nor Swami Satsangi, much less Swami Satyananda, is organizing this tantric festival of Sat Chandi. The priest will be a kanya, the caterer will be a kanya, the singer will be a kanya, the controller of every ritual of this yajna will be a kanya. They will be our hosts. This is the most ancient concept of Shakti tantra.

AWAKENING OF CONSCIOUSNESS

I have selected the kanyas to be the hosts of this event, because this is a very important year when you will remember and remind everyone of the day when man jumped out of his animal consciousness and began to remember that he is a man. That was the day when he discovered fire, and knew it was fire. Fire is eternal. Fire existed before the advent of man, but man did not know how to use it. Animals did not know how to use it. Nobody understood what fire was.

Fire was the first form of God that man realized. Prior to that he was ignorant of time, he was ignorant of space, he was ignorant of everything. He only knew how to sleep, how to be afraid, how to create progeny, how to eat, nothing beyond that. He had no knowledge, no *jnana*, through which he could connect himself to the things around him. The first real day was when man connected with something beyond himself, with fire. Thus the day our ancestors connected with fire, *agni*, millions and millions of years ago, is an immortal and unforgettable day for us. Therefore, the *Rig Veda*, the most ancient book of the Hindus, begins with the word 'agni' – *Agnim ile purohitam*. The first mantra, the first word, was agni.

The second thing that man discovered was grain. Thereafter, he became enlightened. Fire and grain are the two eternal principles. The tradition of yajna began from that day. Thank you God for giving us fire! Thank you God for giving us grain! This yajna reminds us of that event which took place many millions of years ago, when our forefathers discovered the use of fire and grain.

Therefore, at the yajna this year, the five traditional grains: wheat, rice, millet, maize and barley, will be offered to Devi. We offer those five grains to the Devi through her most beautiful form, which is the kanya. When the grain becomes consecrated after being offered to the Cosmic Mother, when it is pure, then it carries the benedictions of the divine. It is not merely food; it is not just grain, not just wheat or rice. It is the consecrated stuff which has been blessed by the Divine Mother, and when I get it, I get its blessings. It is like the offering of bread and wine in the Christian Mass. This is the Mass of the Devi tantra, the Shakti tantra, where you are offered grain.

Some of you will be given rice. Some of you will be given barley. Of course, you have rice and barley at home. I am not giving you anything in charity, because charity is the mother of poverty. I am not talking of charity! I am talking of *prasad*, blessings. When a mother gives something to her child, she is not being charitable. It is her love, it is her compassion, it is her care.

Prasad of grains will be given to everyone, from the neighbouring villagers to those who have come from far away. For Devi, there is no concept of rich and poor, everyone is her child, whether the richest of the rich or the poorest of the poor. If all are children of God, all are children of Devi.

I came here today to explain this to you because it is the most important part of the yajna. You have not come here to see me for blessings or advice. You have come here to receive the blessings of Devi. You need her grace only. Remember this. I will see you all on the final day, after the poornahuti. Until then I don't want to come between you and Devi. Try to

26

make direct contact with Devi in these five days. I have told you the medium for that – the *bal sundaris*, the beautiful children. Live with this *bhava*, this feeling, for five days. The organizers of this yajna, the kanyas, will welcome you tomorrow. To sum up, I am not the host, Swami Niranjan is not the host, nor are the sannyasins. We are all servants here. The Cosmic Mother, through her most beautiful form, the kanya, will be your host for the five days of the yajna. Remember this important point.

WORSHIP OF THE MOTHER

Worship of the Mother is a very ancient culture, which was born with civilization. Worship of the Mother was not introduced by any religion, it was not taught by any canon. It is natural for a child to love his mother. You don't have to teach a child to love his mother because it is in the scriptures, because it is in the *Gita*, the upanishads, the *Bible* or the *Koran*. Love for mother is intrinsic to a child. It is so natural, so spontaneous, so primitive, so total.

From ancient times, right from the beginning of creation, it is the mother who has given birth to the child, not the father. Not only in the history of mankind, but even in the history of God, in the history of all universes and planets, it is the woman who has given birth to the child. Therefore, she was the first person the child knew, not the father. When he was an infant, when he was a child, when he was a boy and when he was a lad, he only knew his mother. The father is a redundant principle, but society has brought him in as a social factor, as a political factor, as an economic factor. The mother is the real friend of the child. Therefore, the worship of Mother is as ancient as mankind.

Some religions denounced mother worship, but not the religion of India where it is considered to be supreme. Mother can never be cruel. Even if she slaps you, it is out of compassion, love and affection. A son may betray his mother, a son may forgo his mother, but a mother cannot and should not repeat

27

the folly of her child. In India, this worship has been prevalent for many thousands of years. We don't call Durga, Kali, Saraswati, Lakshmi, etc. by the name Goddess, we always use the word Devi. *Devi* means luminous, illumined, lustrous, the light that is within. You are all Devi. You are all fortunate.

KANYA WORSHIP

The concept of the kanya is unparalleled in man's philosophy. The discovery that a young virgin was capable of symbolizing and representing the Cosmic Mother was made by a rishi. Could you ever think of your little daughter as the replica of the Mother? No. The idea did not come to the people, only to those *rishis*, the great seers, who saw very clearly. Just as you see greed in money, passion in a woman, fear in a ghost or tiger, why can't you similarly see the goddess in the kanyas? Why do you need to be convinced? Why should I convince you? It is your daily experience that where there is money, there is greed. Money represents greed. The replica of greed is money. The replica of passion is a woman. The replica of fear is a tiger. The replicas of Devi are here. You don't have to prove it. It is as simple as that!

It is written in the upanishads that a person who is innocent, who lives like a child, behaves like a fool among fools, like a scholar among scholars, like a young man among girls, is called an *avadhoota*. These girls are very simple and innocent. Up to the age of puberty they don't know the jugglery of sensual life. There are many who even after puberty remain a virgin mentally and spiritually. Once puberty approaches, the whole system within the body, within the structure and psychology of the mind changes, and manifests in the emotional actions and reactions. Kanya worship is a most important part of Shakti tantra. I have been waiting for this moment. I feel very happy and I want you to feel very happy also, because you are being presented with a new concept, you are being initiated into a new philosophy of life where a little girl can be the replica of the Devi.

28

ASHRAM

Ashrams are a very important part of the Indian psyche. The institution of ashram has existed here for thousands of years. No matter which religion came to India, the ashram tradition was kept alive. Whether it was Buddhism, Jainism, Christianity, Islam, Vaishnavism or Shaivism that became prominent, ashram life continued to be a very important aspect of society. The ashram tradition of sannyasins has continued uninterruptedly.

Even right now, millions of young men and women are attached to one ashram or the other, the Brahma Kumaris, Ramakrishna Mission, Rajneesh, and so on. Adolescents, adults and old people all go to these ashrams and stay there until they find their path. For millions suffering from hopelessness and despondency, the ashrams are like hospices. Many people leave their businesses, homes and parents and go to ashrams. But of these millions, sooner or later, most leave. They go away because they find their path. The percentage of those who stay on, shave their heads and live as sannyasins for life is very small. Nevertheless, it is good to stay at an ashram for any period of time and at any age, as it helps overcome one's negative propensities. The ashrams are a very strong limb of Indian society. If all ashrams were closed down by law today, the number of criminals would go up.

Acceptance is the core
There are millions of ashrams in India, big and small. They are able to survive because the Indian mind by its very nature helps ashrams. Every businessman, corporate house and individual who has a little money will donate to ashrams. It is natural for them, it is ingrained in them. If you were to ask them for donations, they would not be inclined to give, but when they are impressed with your work, you do not have to ask. This has been my experience. People only see whether Swami Satyananda is doing work which is good for society or not. Whether in Rishikesh, Munger, Rikhia or other places, I never asked.

An ashram is not run on a few dollars or rupees; it runs on people's acceptance. If an institution is not accepted, let it die. An institution which is not useful for, or is not serving society, which does not run on the principles of an ashram, should die. Those who run ashrams should remember that a sannyasin has no private life. He has no private account or land. I have never opened a bank account. I have never signed a cheque. I don't own property. If I have to leave this ashram today, I will leave barely with what's on me. I don't even have the money to purchase a train ticket. That is how a sannyasin has to live. And for such people, Indians will do anything.

Generating an atmosphere
One who runs an ashram should live like a *snataka*, like a celibate free of worldly instincts. An ashram has to have an atmosphere. You have to create such an atmosphere that when people come there, they inhale peace and energy. The ashram may be made of bricks and mortar, but there has to be an energy cycle in it. That is what we have been doing in the ashrams of India for thousands of years.

30

There is an episode in the *Brihadaranyaka Upanishad*. Yajnavalkya, the great muni and guru of King Janaka, wanted to renounce, go to the forest and take sannyasa. He called his two wives, Maitreyi and Katyayani. He said to them, "I want to divide my property between the two of you." Katyayani quietly took her share of the property, but Maitreyi said, "What will I do with property? Give me something which is spiritual." Such has to be the attitude of a person who lives within the precincts of an ashram. The ashram has to be like a temple, even if it consists of just one room. This tradition has been in India from the vedic period, and it should be maintained.

You have all come here to breathe in the spiritual atmosphere. You experience a spiritual atmosphere here because the people around are poor, the swamis here are very good, and I am here. The first, the second and the last purpose of my life has been to live a spiritual life. When I was eighteen or nineteen, I woke up and decided to live a spiritual life. Ultimately, I realized that spiritual life lies within you. Wherever you are, you can lead a spiritual life.

In an ashram, there should be sattwic enjoyment. Every ashram, whether big or small, should celebrate important events from time to time. The ashram must have an atmosphere of sattwic mirth and joy. Not dullness, not a Sunday face. When you are living a spiritual life, you can dance, sing and enjoy, but it has to be sattwic enjoyment.

What is sattwic enjoyment, rajasic enjoyment and tamasic enjoyment? When your enjoyment depends on external objects, it is *rajasic* enjoyment. When your enjoyment depends on your own self, *atmananda*, it is called *sattwic* enjoyment. When you are singing kirtan or bhajan, or chanting the Mahamrityunjaya mantra, the joy that you experience does not come from an external source. It comes from within, it is independent, it is sattwic ananda. So, create an ashram as a place for atmananda.

Shram

There are certain rules that must be observed within an ashram. Just as the chief attribute of salt is saltiness, of honey sweetness and of chilli sharpness, the chief element of an ashram is shram. *Shram* means to live like a labourer. 'Labour' as a word is often used in the context of socialism. The tradition of the ashram, too, is socialist; an ashram is not a capitalist entity.

I lived in the ashram of my guru sixty years ago, Sri Rama lived in an ashram in Treta yuga, Sri Krishna lived in an ashram in Dwapara yuga. At all these places, one had to labour. The story goes that Krishna once went to the forest with Sudama to chop wood. They got caught in a storm and had to spend the night there. Sudama's bundle of puffed rice was all they had for food. At Rishi Vashishtha's ashram, Sri Rama would feed the cows and tend the plants. However, along with all this work, the ashramites also receive knowledge of the scriptural sciences.

Formal study is essential to life, but every child should be given knowledge that relates to his life. You study physics and chemistry, but you do not know how to keep your mind under control. You may score ninety-five percent in physics, but if you remain a loser in life, what is the use of such study? I am not saying that studying is not important. It is important to make a living, but you must know more about life. When I say life, I mean one's body and mind. People don't know who they are, they while away their time in gossip. You should stay away from such useless things.

A disciple, an aspirant must be receptive. Plastic won't absorb water, but if you pour water into a sponge, it will soak it up. To learn anything, the aspirant should also be receptive like a sponge. And to become receptive, you need to do physical labour in an ashram. When you perform shram, every part of the body from the head to the toes is managed, the way a machine is completely repaired. Every part is cleaned; all the nadis, granthis and muscles of the body are cleansed through shram.

32

The food that you eat is believed to contain all the necessary nutrients, yet you fall sick. So it is not necessary that strength-producing food is health-producing too. More than the kind of food, it is the assimilation of food in the body that is important. This means that every part, every nutrient of the food must reach the right place. This is the merit of labour. In the villages, people rise at four a.m. and walk to faraway fields to evacuate their bowels, they bathe in the pond and sweep their own homes. What do they eat? Salt and rice. But they have the strength to carry bricks, plough fields and carry loads the whole day through. I am a witness to their state of health.

We have a very good dispensary here, for which medicines come from Australia, New Zealand, Mumbai, Delhi and other places, but we have to give away many of these medicines in Deoghar, because they don't get used. The people here just don't fall sick. We give away all the medicines for diabetes. Diabetes does not exist here. They get tuberculosis, coughs, colds, fever or skin disease. They don't get the big diseases. A few medicines, quinine and injections are good enough to cure them. And they don't consume Vitamin A, B, C and D. They eat whatever they get.

Observing the rules

For howsoever long you stay in an ashram, get up early, try to help as much as you can, and learn kirtan. Whenever you get the time, come again. The ashram does not belong to anyone. The ashram teaches just one thing: observe decorum. You need to observe decorum not only in the ashram, but also at home. Decorum means to stay within boundaries. Nobody eats food in the toilet, and nobody uses the bedroom as a toilet. This is called decorum, to do that which is appropriate to a given place. To smoke within the ashram, for example, is not decorous. No one stops you from smoking outside, but don't do it within the ashram.

You should know what is appropriate and inappropriate in an ashram. Decorum is the basis of discipline. The day such discipline breaks down, society will collapse. Discipline is the foundation of life. Discipline in Sanskrit is called *anushasana*, to rule over oneself. It is not self-control, it is to rule over oneself. Without discipline, you cannot run people, the family or the country. Discipline determines decorum.

There are four ashramas of life – brahmacharya, grihastha, vanaprastha and sannyasa. This is sannyasa ashrama. It is not necessary that only sannyasins should live here, yet it is sannyasa ashrama. In *grihastha* or householder ashrama, everyone lives according to their social background, but the grihastha ashrama instincts should not enter the ashram premises. I don't mean that grihastha ashrama is bad; it simply should not be mixed up with sannyasa ashrama.

If you come to the ashram, live by its rules or go away. If you don't know how to swim, don't step into deep waters. Whether you come to the ashram for a health management course, sannyasa course, as a guest, detective or thief, you will have to observe the decorum of the ashram. If you don't, you will be thrown out.

CHILDREN

Educating children

Children are the prospect of the future. They will have to be prepared not just in the context of one country, but in the context of the whole world. Whatever you earn, should be used to the fullest extent to give your children a good and modern education. This means that the principal part of your earnings should be spent on their education. It is essential that children advance in their studies. If a child is not interested in studying, don't take him from school to make him work at something else. Nowadays, education is of many kinds: sports and modelling are also a kind of education.

Sportspeople earn from eight to eighty million rupees a year. Whether or not people know the name of their prime minister, they know the models. Modelling, too, earns a good income, and it also gives a boost to the textile industry. Therefore, education should be such that children are in tune with the present and future society. The future society will be a hi-tech one. The dreams of the current generation are hi-tech too. They may want to take a ride on a bullock cart or elephant for a change, but what they really want is a Mercedes car.

Nowadays, girls have many options too. Earlier, in every society, whether eastern or western, there was only one option for girls: grow up and get married. The options of studying or setting up a business did not exist. Today all these options are open. A woman can become president, chief of the army staff, a scientist, space traveller or revolutionary. She can pick up a gun, she can do anything. The tradition of differentiating between boys and girls should be ended, and if the affluent take the lead in this cause, it will be better. The poor cannot do this work. There is a saying, "Who will bell the cat?" Only a cat can bell a cat, not a mouse. So start this process.

The amount budgeted for the education of a girl should be the same as the amount budgeted for the education of a boy. Through education, girls should fulfil their dreams of becoming something. They can become businesswomen, industrialists or social workers, anything. Along with establishing a career, those who wish to set up house should do so. This is a question of understanding. It seems illogical that parents should fix a girl's marriage. I have to get married, but you will get it fixed. How strange! If I wish to get married, the choice should be mine, not my father's. This irrational method that has continued till now should be ended, and the one who wishes to get married should be given the right to choose.

The one who wants to eat should choose whether he wishes to eat rasagulla or chamcham. The one who wishes to wear clothes should choose whether she wishes to wear trousers or a sari. If the social aspirations of children are not left up to them but dictated by us, we will carry their burden as well. We will feel burdened and the children will feel

35

suffocated their whole life through. This is what happened in the past with our mothers and wives. From the psychological point of view, they were a complex-ridden sex. Society must give its children the chance to express their talent if the country is to progress.

It is the job of parents to provide an opportunity for their children. 'Opportunity' means prospects. If you have a shoe or textile business, you may expect that your child will take that up too – it is natural, every person looks for a successor – but that is not offering a prospect. If you try to honestly assess whether the child is better off looking after the shop or doing something else, you are offering a prospect. Prospect comes into effect when the child goes forward on his own quest and returns something through the quest. He will then find a place in history, his quest will find a place in history. Not only that, he may also earn royalties worth millions of rupees. In today's age, name and fame are not enough; one has to have money too. Today's age is the age of balance. Along with fame, money is also necessary. The two go side by side.

So, parents should put their children on the path of education, give them the chance to grow and study. This is the extent of your responsibility towards your children. When they grow up, they can look after their own future.

Change

The future generation depends on how you train the children. Every generation has its own peculiarities, difficulties, problems, likes and dislikes. Your children don't like what you like and don't dislike what you dislike. What you dislike is what they like. This is called change, and it is natural. Every generation has to change just as day has to change into night and night has to change into day. Autumn has to give way to winter and winter has to give way to summer. If there were just one generation or one culture, it would become monotonous. Change has to come about. And the most natural change is generational change.

36

Kanyas and batuks

At Rikhia, we have adopted almost five to six thousand young boys and girls, *kanyas* and *batuks*, virgins and celibates. All day long, they swarm around the ashram like bees. They go home only at night because their huts are not very inspiring, as they are poor people. They speak very good English, and they are learning computers at the ashram. In two months they have learnt what students in the big cities learn in two years. The older ones among

them have started teaching the younger ones. Their maximum age is thirteen. In the ashram, we allow girls only up to the age of thirteen. After thirteen, they retire to make way for more children.

We don't know what the future of these children is. It lies in the hands of God. We are doing our karma, our duty. Originally, the classes started with just one girl, and now there are so many. I think they, as well as their parents, are very happy. One thing is very important; we don't deal with anyone in the village except the children. Through them we deal with the entire family.

We have started Sanskrit classes for the boys. All these little scoundrels are studying the *Bhagavad Gita*. They are so energetic, so aggressive, so all over the place – managing fifty girls equals managing one boy! But I don't see it negatively. Sri Krishna was like this. He used to create

37

problems in the whole village. Every day the people of the village would complain about him to his mother. She would try to give him a beating, but he would run away and say, "They are all telling lies, I'm such a good boy. They don't like me, so they tell you new stories about me every day. I have never been to their houses. I go to graze my cows." But he was at the centre of all the troubles. He would break the gopi girls' earthen water pots and steal their clothes while they were bathing in the river. When they would request him to return the clothes, he would say, "Come and get them."

The bhaktas of Krishna interpret the incident philosophically. The *gopi* represents the senses. Clothes represent the subject or object, *vishaya*. They are the samskaras, gunas, properties or attachments of the senses. The senses are covered with the attachments. If you want to have the perception of God, you should come without the coverings. Go to God naked. The bhaktas of Krishna believe, the Lord says, "Just as I have asked you to come without your clothes, in the same way I ask you to come in purity before me. Don't come with your habits, hang-ups, obsessions, name, caste, sex and religion. Come as a jiva."

ENERGY FIELDS

I went to Vaishno Devi and it felt as if I had brought back an energy field from there, but a few months later it disappeared.

There are two kinds of aspirants – stupid and crooked. In Sanskrit, the stupid are called *moodha*, idiotic, and the crooked are called *shatha*, wicked. When the stupid aspirant comes within the periphery of an energy field, it has no effect on him. It is the same as not being able to pass electricity through wood because it is a bad conductor. The crooked aspirant, however, is a good conductor. When he receives *satsang*, the company of the pious, when he is within an energy field, he is affected.

Crooked aspirants are also of two kinds. One is affected by being within an energy field, but resumes his crooked nature on emerging from it. The relationship of the other kind of crooked aspirant with a pure energy field is like the relationship between iron and the philosopher's stone. The philosopher's stone can convert iron into gold, but it does not turn iron into the philosopher's stone. Tulsidas wrote on this subject in the *Ramacharitamanas*:

> *Shatha sudharahin satasangatee paaee,*
> *Paarasa parasa kudhaatu suhaaee.*

Just as iron turns into gold with the touch of the philosopher's stone, a wicked man too transforms through the company of the pious.

Kudhatu means iron that turns into gold. This is true. A crooked person can change. That is why it has been said that everyone should go to an ashram, place of pilgrimage or satsang every now and then. If this is not possible, then in your own house, for fifteen minutes, half an hour or an hour, once a month or a few days in the year, create such an environment that the energy field that you are talking about is created. That energy field in fact exists within you, within every person.

There is an energy field within us. I am speaking from the point of view of science now. You might have heard the name of a Russian couple called Kirlian. They conducted an experiment and discovered that human beings are surrounded by an energy field. The halo that you see around Rama or Krishna in their pictures is the energy field that surrounds every individual. It increases and decreases, stays for a very long time and disappears too. In fact, every object that you touch has an energy field. This is a vast subject.

Every individual is an energy field in himself, and this energy field can be expanded as well as contracted. You do not need any other energy field. You may go to a guru, a saint or on a pilgrimage and come within the periphery of an external energy field, but on returning, that energy field slowly diminishes. The energy field that you went into at Vaishno Devi was that of the Devi. It was a manifested energy field; you are an unmanifest energy field. The divine energy field that lies within you is contracted. So try to make it manifest.

Some people say that the energy field within lies in the mind, some say in the heart, and some say in mooladhara chakra. It is difficult to see it, but it is through this magnetic energy that many people compel thousands and millions to follow them like the Pied Piper of Hamelin. Hitler took all of Germany within his energy field. Wherever Mahatma Gandhi went, a storm followed him. He had such a strong influence that entire villages would walk behind him. He was just a lawyer from Gujarat who went abroad and then returned to India. People did not follow him because he was working for the independence of India, but because his magnetic energy field had expanded to such an extent that they found themselves inadvertently drawn to him.

The energy field exists within every person; it is not possible to lose it. You may think that you received it from someone or somewhere and then lost it, but that's because you cannot manifest your own energy field. To do this, the medium will have to be your worldly life. Marriage, food, home, society and work are the mediums. They are not the aim, just as the train is the medium and not the destination. Life, family, body, yoga, copulation, joy and sorrow are mediums. Whoever exists in this world is a medium. This is the thought that you should walk with.

One who considers this world as the medium never suffers. Suffering is felt by one who considers life to be the destination. Ramakrishna Paramahamsa and Ramana Maharishi considered their soul as the foundation and therefore they became gods. You, too, can become God. A normal person does not become God because he considers his life as the goal. If you do not consider your life, son, wife, husband as the goal, you will find that nothing ever goes wrong. The pain of neither the body nor the mind is felt any longer.

GOD

Two paths

To realize God, you need not worship statues. No one has said that only by worshipping a stone image of Shiva will you realize him. If you want to find God without any medium at all, you can certainly do so. All the saints have said this. They have described two paths to reach God: *vihangam marga*, the path of the bird, and *pipilika marga*, the path of the ant. If you are a bird, you may fly straight from where you are. You do not need a bus or car. If you have wings, fly like a bird and you will certainly reach that supreme spirit and realize him. But those who do not have wings can use the method of the ant. The ant has to traverse the whole distance.

The path of the ant is for those who are caught up in the attachments and illusions of the world, who are under the sway of their mind, the gunas, likes and dislikes, who feel happy with one thing and sad with another. Such people need some kind of a base to realize God. This base is the mind.

The mind as the base

With the mind as the base, you internalize, go within. The supreme spirit that you wish to realize may exist externally, pervade the whole world and creation, but it exists within you too, so the mind is used as the base to realize it. But you must properly understand what kind of base the mind is.

Say, you pick a rose from a garden. The rose is separate from you. You see it as an object and it is separate from you. When you close your eyes and try to visualize the rose, you see the rose within. This rose is different from the rose you plucked from the garden. Mark my words: the rose that you have placed on your desk and the rose that you are looking at within your mind are different. One is *para*, external, and the other is internal. What you see within is not a rose blossom, but with the image of the rose blossom as the base,

41

you are seeing yourself. When you worship the images of Rama, Shiva or Devi in a temple, when you close your eyes and meditate on them, what you see within at that point is not them, but you. You are the image of the supreme spirit, you are its resplendence. Assume that you close your eyes and see me. The image of 'me' that you see by closing your eyes is not me, but you. Until you grasp this matter, you will not find the answer to your questions.

Realization

The supreme spirit makes itself attainable. The base and the external guru are left outside; the guru who shines within is your own self. The statue of Shiva that you look at is you. He is not the Shiva residing at Baidyanathdham or Vishwanath temple. That which is within is real. What is realization of mind, consciousness and self? People focus their mental energy on the image of a rose or shivalingam. Slowly, they stabilize their mind on a symbol. After some days, that experience is lost, it goes away, nothing and no one remains. In that nothingness, the image of God exists and does not exist at the same time.

How can I tell you whether God has an image or not? No

one has been able say this. No one has had the last word on God. They have not been able to say that God is not stone. Has anyone said that? If someone says that God is not an image, what proof do they have? What is the proof that God has a form or is formless? No one has ever been able to prove either. A Muslim cannot give proof of Allah, a Christian cannot give proof of God and I cannot give proof of the soul. God is beyond proof, he is unprovable, immeasurable.

42

GOD'S HOME

There is only one place in the world where Christ has his own house, his own cottage – it is Christ Kutir here in Rikhia. *Kutir* means cottage. It is a very ancient Indian concept. A kutir is not a church; a church is a sanctum-sanctorum. It is not a temple; a temple is a place where God is worshipped. Christ Kutir is the place where he lives. A place of worship and a place of residence are two different things, just as the place of work and the place to live are different. You may spend eight or ten hours in your office, but that is not your home. Similarly, a sanctum-sanctorum is not a permanent place of God. The permanent place is where one rests, eats, where one is informal, where one lives as one wants to.

When I established Christ Kutir here, the thought in my mind was that Christ must have his own home. He was working in a factory in Israel. He works in different factories, in different churches. He goes there for a short while just as you go to the office. He goes there on Sundays, and then he returns. But where does he return to? If you ever meet him, ask him to come to Rikhia. He has a nice place here.

Christ Kutir is not the only place in Rikhia where God lives. There is also Ganesha Kutir, the cottage for Ganesha. There is Raghunath Kutir, the cottage for Raghunath. Our gods and goddesses don't have any home. Wherever they go, they are on duty. Shiva is always being offered water; the poor fellow is sitting underwater twenty-four hours a day. Where is God's home? God has his home at two places. Ganeshji, for example, has his home at two places – here in Ganesha Kutir and within all your hearts. However, it is very painful for him to live in your heart because it is dirty. Just as you would find it difficult to live in a house which is full of plastic, spit and flies, God finds it painful to live in a heart that is dirty. So Ganeshji lives here in Ganesha Kutir, and showers abundant grace upon us. Raghunathji too has showered his grace on us, and so has Christ.

Grace

It was through the grace of Christ that I was able to conquer so many Christian nations and hoist the flag of yoga there. When there is grace, the lame are able to climb a mountain, the dumb begin to speak and the blind begin to see. I was born in a farmer's family, but there is not a country or town I did not take yoga to. This does not happen through one's own strength. Tulsidas has said:

> *Jaakee charana kamala bandau Hari raaee*
> *Jaakee kripaa pangu giri langhai*
> *Andhe ko saba kuchha darshaaee*
> *Baharo sunai, mooka puni bole*
> *Ranka chale sira chatra dharaaee*
> *Charana kamala bandau Hari raaee.*

I prostrate at the lotus feet of Lord Hari by whose grace a lame person can cross mountains, a blind person can see, a deaf person can hear, a mute person can speak and a penniless person becomes a king.

No matter how weak a person is, no matter what family he is born into, whether he is attached to desires like Surdas, whether he runs after a woman like Tulsidas, once the grace of God descends, iron turns into gold, coal into diamonds, Tulsi into Tulsidas and the blind into Surdas.

To receive God's grace, however, his home should be kept clean. To make God dwell in your heart, to make sure that he continues to remain there and bless you and your home, it is essential that you clean your heart. It is difficult to explain the meaning of cleaning the heart. How would you know that your heart is clean? Ramakrishna Paramahamsa used to say, where there is dirt, flies come; where there is wealth, thieves come, but if there is a beautiful garden with a lake, blooming lotuses and chirping birds, everyone goes there. Similarly, you can tell what kind of a heart you have by the people you attract.

Heart and mind

The heart and the mind are two different things. The heart is about feelings and the mind is about thoughts. Thoughts are born from the mind and feelings from the heart. If your heart is pure, your thoughts will be positive. If you have negative thoughts, thoughts of fear, criticism, violence, passion, anger and jealousy, something is wrong with your feelings.

If your heart is clean, your thoughts will be free from jealousy, greed, lust, anger, vengeance, worry, fear and insecurity. That is the barometer of life and of purity. Thoughts don't make you a good person; it is the heart, it is your feelings that make you a good person. You may read an inspiring book about Buddha, Christ or Swami Vivekananda and have good thoughts. It's nothing. You may appreciate the ideas in the book, but you can't feel them. It is the feeling that is important; it is the feeling that is the basis of bhakti, too, not the mind.

Basis of bhakti

The basis of bhakti is the heart, not the mind. The basis of bhakti is emotion. Bhakti cannot exist without emotion, just as anger, fear, jealousy, worry, joy and sorrow cannot exist without emotion. To experience bhakti, however, you must redirect your emotions from the inauspicious to the auspicious path; you must take the flow of the river of desires to an auspicious course. It has been said:

Shubhabhyam ashubhabhyam vahanti vasana sarita.

Between the auspicious and the inauspicious, flows the river of desires. ·

We call the river of desires 'emotion'. We do not see this river, but we feel it. Emotions flow within us like a river. We can control this river, change its course, turn it into a channel, take it to the fields and generate electricity through it. The river that was flooding the fields, villages and habitation, and damaging its own banks, has now become creative. In the

45

same way, the emotion through which you become angry, through which passion and jealousy are generated within you, which causes you to shoot someone, can be made to change its course. However, you cannot have half of your emotional self here and half there. You cannot experience anger and bhakti at the same time. The rule of fifty-fifty does not work. There needs to be one hundred percent sublimation of emotions, a complete change of course. What will be achieved through this? Grace.

After all, what was Swami Vivekananda? He could have become a lawyer, but instead he became a national figure, an inspiration for thousands of people. I belonged to an average family, but my guru changed the entire direction of my emotions and life. It has happened this way because it is God's will. God goes with those who have sublimated their emotions, who have cleansed their heart. Even a jnani has negative thoughts, but he sends them off to the septic tank, he disposes of them.

Managing the gunas

There are three gunas: sattwa, rajas and tamas. The entire creation is under the control of the gunas. You may contain sattwa guna in half measure, someone else in quarter, three-quarters, and so on. The one who can go beyond the three gunas is a liberated soul. Such people are *videhamuktas*, *jivanmuktas* (free of the body), and they live in a different realm. They exist beyond *shoonya*, void. Kabir has described the four stages of existence: *jagrat* (wakefulness), *swapna* (dreaming), *sushupti* (deep sleep) and *turiya* (super-con-sciousness). The fourth state, turiya, is very high.

Most people live within the three gunas. It is possible to manage the gunas by living according to dharma. *Dharma* is an attitude, it is effort, it is day-to-day life, it is the interaction between people, between individuals and society, husband and wife, friends and enemies. Rituals do not constitute dharma. They are part of bhakti, they come under karma-kanda and tantra. Dharma is different; a dharmic life begins

46

with life itself, just as bhakti begins with emotion. So, the three gunas have to be managed through dharma. Just as you throw away rubbish, clean the sheets and cobwebs, you have to work with the gunas too. The gunas exist in your house as well – the objects of purity, enjoyment and disposal represent the gunas. The way you manage them is the way you need to manage your heart.

Surrender

When the heart has become pure through proper management, God will live in it. Then you will find that your destiny, the very direction of your life rests in the hands of God. It is said,

Dinabandhu dinanath, meri dori tere hath.

O friend and lord of the poor, you hold the string of my life.

Whether God takes you to the butcher's or turns you into a deity in a temple, you have given over the strings of your life to him. If you completely surrender to God, nothing is impossible, but don't put conditions on the act of surrender. Don't say, "I worship you, so look after me." He is omniscient; he controls your mind, prana, limbs, your life and death. Is he so foolish that you need to tell him to remove your sorrows? He has given sorrow, joy, wealth, poverty, illness. He is all-powerful, all-pervading. He has the three gunas of omnipotence, omniscience and omnipresence. He is present everywhere. He knows everything. He can do anything. In principle you accept all this, yet you doubt him. If you truly believe that he is omnipresent, omniscient and omnipotent, you would not feel the need to ask him for anything. You would leave it up to him.

Union

The building I live in is called Gauri-Ganesha. The relationship between Radha and Krishna depicts *madhurya bhava* (the emotion between the lover and the beloved). Subhadra, Balarama and Krishna's relationship depicts *sneha bhava* (the

47

emotion between brother and sister). Yashoda and Krishna, Kaushalya and Rama, Mary and Christ depict *vatsalya bhava* (the emotion between child and parent). These are different forms of expressing bhakti. I think Gauri and Ganesha portray a very nice example of vatsalya bhava, so I called my house Gauri-Ganesha and placed their statue here.

God is tied to you through the thread of love. What is the meaning of love? It is not what you see on the television. It is the term for an emotion where two opposite elements assume union. Kabir has said:

Prema na baree upajai, prema na haata bikaaya
Raajaa parjaa jehi ruchai, sheesha deya le jai.

Love does not grow in the fields. Love is not sold in the marketplace. Love can be acquired by one, whether king or commoner, who is ready to offer his head for it.

When a merger between two opposite poles takes place, that is love. According to physics, every object has a positive and a negative pole. They are known as *desha* (space) and *kaala* (time). When they come towards each other, they merge in the nucleus. In physics it is called merger; we call it yoga.

48

The union that is achieved in dhyana or in the worship of the divine is also between two opposite elements – Purusha and Prakriti, paramatma and jivatma. These opposite elements have been ascribed different names. We often refer to the union of the material and the spiritual, the mind and the spirit. The mind and its thoughts are material, gross entities because the mind has emerged out of the five elements. So it unites with that which is not material. The supreme spirit is not a material object; it is a transcendental and omnipresent principle. A material object cannot be omnipresent; it can exist only at one place at a given time. But the supreme spirit is omnipresent; it exists everywhere at all times. You may try to raise the level of the mind through mantra, make it subtler, internalize it, but it is a material object. The merger of that material object with the supreme spirit is called yoga, union between two opposite elements. This is the meaning of love too. Love should not be understood through a limited definition; it should not be understood as rapture and emotion alone. Love is the term for an awareness, remembrance, madness. It is said in the *Ramacharitamanas*:

Kaamihi naari piaari jimi lobhihi priya jimi daama
Timi Raghunaatha nirantara priya laagahu mohi Raama.

May you ever be so dear to me, Rama, as a woman is dear to a lustful man, and as lucre is dear to the greedy, O lord of the Raghus.

Solitude

I live alone in Gauri-Ganesha. People try to live in solitude, but they are not able to. Just as the stomach needs food, an individual needs society, friendship and love. For many years I tried to live without these, tried to live alone, tried hard, tried in Rishikesh, but it did not happen. I was always given duties. I once said to Swami Sivananda, "Swamiji, I want to live alone." He said, "Yes, live alone while working." I said,

49

"But I have to work with others." He replied, "Why do you worry about others? You live alone, keep yourself in solitude, *alakh niranjan.*" But it was not possible. I would get into fights, get attached, feel bad – this is the effect of company. This will not happen in solitude. In solitude, there is neither me nor you, but love and quarrels go hand in hand with companionship.

After leaving Rishikesh, for many years I was travelling all over the place. Then I came to Rikhia. It became difficult here too. When I came, there was complete solitude the whole day through. Now Rikhia is changing. I am thinking I should leave Gauri-Ganesha, too, and go off to Uttarakhand now. A small cottage has been made there. I might be able to live in solitude there.

GURU

The beginning of faith

A human being has two things: intelligence and faith. It was through intelligence that he learnt about God, but it was through faith that he experienced God. Not knowledge, but experience comes about through faith. Just as love, enmity, jealousy, joy and sorrow are not the stuff of the intellect but of experience, faith is also a matter of experience. The basis of the intellect is analysis. The upanishads may have been written with the help of intelligence, but faith is such a substance that it accepts even that which is invisible. After all, has anyone seen anger? No. But anger exists. This is a matter of faith. You do not need to see faith, you need to experience faith. Therefore, at the very beginning of *Ramacharitamanas*, it has been said,

Bhavaaneeshankarau vande shraddhaavishvaasarupinau,
Yaabhyaam vinaa na pashyaanti siddhaah svaantahsthameeshwaram.

Without shraddha and vishwas, faith and deep conviction, even great siddhas cannot achieve spiritual attainment.

A *siddha*, an accomplished person, too cannot see the God within, the one who is so close to him, if he does not have faith and belief. To experience God, faith and belief are prime necessities, and the beginning of faith and belief is through the guru. The guru and the disciple are strangers to each other at the beginning, they may come from different places. However, the disciple finds faith in the guru. He starts learning the A, B, C, D of faith, and through continuous practice he develops faith. In this faith, he sees the shadow, the reflection and splendour of God.

Even a siddha has to practise faith in the guru. But prior to the guru, one has to practise faith in one's parents. You do not know who your father is. You cannot know who your father is until there is a DNA test, but you believe that this person is your father because your faith says so. To believe that your father is your father for your entire life, or to accept a stranger as your wife or husband is faith. This is the first rung of school, kindergarten. First you practise faith and belief in your own house, then in the guru and finally in God. When, by practising it in different things, the faith becomes strong, clear and divine, when it is generated from a pure mind and heart, you see God. Then God, who was defined in different ways by different people, becomes apparent to you.

Faith and belief are essential, though intelligence has its own place. Once someone asked me, "Swamiji, why do people worship the idols of gods and goddesses?" I said that at the level of intelligence, this may seem odd. After all, how can a piece of stone be God? How can a piece of paper be God? How can a person who eats and sleeps be guru and God? The intelligence may question all this, but when it comes to faith, then a stone is indeed God, a leaf is God, a tree is God. Faith can establish anything as God.

Faith is the biggest power. If you do not have faith, then forget about God. Don't even talk about him, because you cannot realize God by talking about him. You can talk about God for years and eons, but nothing will be achieved through that. Ramakrishna Paramahamsa used to say that you can keep writing "Water, water, water" on a piece of paper, but you cannot get water by wringing that piece of paper. You only wrote 'water' on the paper, you did not soak it in water. Experiencing God is equally simple.

Crisis point

The guru-disciple relationship is a very important relationship. To begin with, it is very difficult to form and if formed, it is very hard to uphold. This is because the guru lives in a body, which means that he eats, sleeps, excretes, speaks and laughs like you do. Observing this, you may question the difference between you and the guru. At that point, the tenacity of your relationship with the guru becomes weak. You think, "Oh, he is just like us, so what is the point." People said the same thing to Lord Buddha. They said, "Lord, what is the difference between you and us? We eat and so do you, we sleep and so do you, we laugh and so do you." When you begin to think like this, the steadfastness of the guru-disciple relationship becomes difficult to maintain.

It is very easy to call someone your guru, but it is very difficult to maintain that relationship. The guru lives the same way as you do. You see no difference between you and him because spiritual illumination cannot be seen. How do you know what I think or do? You only look at what I wear, eat and drink, how I sleep, laugh, what I keep, and so on. No one can see what lies within. Who will look at what lies within? After all, only a Shakespeare can understand a Shakespeare. If you have the eyes to see, only then will you understand what lies within the guru. But you do not have the eyes, therefore the doubts come.

The greatest crisis between a guru and disciple takes place when the disciple is not able to stabilize his relationship with the guru. He may have established a relationship, but he cannot stabilize it. Therefore, many times gurus and disciples fall apart. So, it is not an easy relationship. It is not as if you have made a guru, now you can go to his ashram and get liberated. There are many crises. There are crises between husband and wife, between brother and sister, and there are crises between guru and disciple too. After all, they are strangers. Like bricks and stones, they come from different places to make a house.

If we get inappropriate thoughts about the guru, what is the reason? How can we remove them?

Once you have accepted someone as your guru, he is your guru, whether you are inappropriate or appropriate. Once you are married to a person, you are married, no matter what thoughts you get. The truth will remain the truth. It is only the imbalance within you that needs to be corrected. Inappropriate thoughts do come to the mind, but the relationship should not become any lesser due to or despite them.

The relationship between a guru and disciple is not physical, social or of the blood. It is not a worldly relationship, such as that between brother and sister, father and son, husband and wife. The guru-disciple relationship is spiritual. The guru becomes the base of your spiritual life. Therefore, this relationship should be maintained well. In the scriptures, twenty-four kinds of gurus have been mentioned. There are different types of gurus. There was one guru who came to India from a different country. He was a great soul, a sadhaka, someone who had the grace of God upon him. His first wife died, and he married a second time. Now, some of his disciples may have had inappropriate thoughts. Not everyone would have, some people are wise, but some would have said, "What kind of a guru is he? He married twice."

If you think about Guruji getting married twice, or the kind of clothes he is wearing and the food he is eating, that he is smoking marijuana and drinking alcohol, these thoughts are occurring in your mind due to your personal reasons. If the reasons were impersonal, wouldn't fingers have been pointed at Sri Krishna too? The inappropriate thoughts in people's minds, which they may speak out or write about in books, are creations of their own minds. They are in the head of the disciple and do not affect the actuality of the guru and should not affect the relationship between the guru and disciple either.

A human being has sense organs in the body. Beyond the sense organs lies the mind, beyond the mind lies the intelligence, and beyond intelligence lies the soul. The mind generates sattwic, rajasic and tamasic thoughts. Let the thoughts come, there is no problem, and there is no solution to this either. If you think inappropriately about the guru, there is no harm. It is the mind that thinks inappropriately, not the soul. The soul never thinks inappropriately.

If inappropriate thoughts come, let them come; the clouds are rumbling now and will disappear in time. Speaking in practical terms, to get the better of your inappropriate thoughts, do three things. Send a yearly dakshina to the guru, whatever you can, with love and devotion. Second, on Guru Poornima, go to him and worship him, and if that is not possible, worship at home only. Third, do japa of the guru mantra regularly. If you have a quarrel with your guru or husband, don't stop eating, bathing and sleeping, and don't leave the husband or guru. Quarrels are normal, but they should not influence your entire life.

When I was eighteen or nineteen years old, I used to go to Nainital on holidays. A Devi temple exists near the lake there, next to which is a peculiar rock. Once I found a yogini there. She was fat, dark and would smoke all day long. I could not understand why she left home if all she wanted to do was to smoke. I was a child, and this was my way of thinking. One day I was sitting there, and a few of her followers came. She started talking and I was stunned. Then I started going to her every day. From morning till evening I would remain there, and every day what I heard would surprise me. I developed such faith in her that I asked her to make me her disciple. She asked me to look for a different guru and eventually went away, but I remember her to this date. So I feel one should not judge a guru by the external environment.

To measure the guru by your own meter is not right either. Every person has a meter, which is his way of thinking. He uses his own yardstick to measure whether the guru is tall, short, fat, good, right, wrong, lawful, etc. This should not happen, because often the gurus who have spiritual wealth keep it hidden. The gurus receive *vibhooti*, divine blessings, or the experience of a part of God. At some time or the other, they would have felt a part of God, maybe in meditation, while bathing, sleeping or walking. It is an experience that comes suddenly, like a flash. Such great souls who have received that light are gurus. However, they keep their attainment hidden, because if they reveal it, they will be robbed. At the Shiva temple, the devotees touch the shivalingam every day, so much so that it almost disappears. The devotees trouble God very much, so God has hidden himself, become attribute-less and formless. Similarly, many gurus keep themselves hidden. What is the way to hide? Smoke a chillum. People will say, what kind of a guru is this, why should the one who has had the perception of God smoke? The guru gets away, and you people get funny thoughts in your head. The loss is yours. So be a bit wary of gurus.

POVERTY

The humble people of the Indian rural community live a life perfectly in balance with nature. They don't disturb nature for their own purpose, sustenance, greed or sensuality. They do not exploit nature, but live with nature. Any community that lives with nature follows a divine path. Nature is not created by divinity, but is a part of divinity. There is silence and simplicity in the lives of those who live with nature.

The poverty that the villagers live in is not self-imposed; it is a result of their situation. Nevertheless, it is a positive thing. Poverty is not a negative thing. It may be a negative thing for the greedy, the exploiters, the cheats and dacoits, but for those who are seeking spiritual life, poverty is not a negative state. In fact, if you want to experience spirituality, live like a poor person even if you are not poor. Reduce your wants, limit your needs and restrict your temptations. This does not go against the tenets of any religion; rather, this is what every religion has been saying for several millennia. There is no end to human desires. Desires will continue to grow. A restriction, limit or brake has to be put on them.

The rural community in Rikhia is very poor. Blessed are the poor! The poor are always meek. Poor people cannot assume arrogance. If they act arrogantly, they will be kicked by the rich. The poor do not have a chance. The only way for them is to be meek. It has been said in the *Bible*, "The meek shall inherit the earth." So, blessed are the meek.

PURUSHARTHA

If everything happens through the will of God, then what is the need for purushartha, self-effort?
No one has been able to give a final answer to this question as yet. So we will only discuss it. The *Bhagavad Gita, Srimad Bhagavatam*, other scriptures and all philosophies discuss this question. If God is the doer, then what is our role? You are looking for a conclusive answer to this question, but you will not find it because your mind is not ready for it. And when you do get the final answer, the questioner would have ceased to exist.

On the basis of my experiences in the eighty years of my life, I can say this. Whatever has happened in my life has not been due to my effort or *purushartha*. Even if I had made no effort, it would have happened. Yet I made the effort, because that in itself was a part of the will of God. This is the important point. God wanted me to achieve and, therefore, it was not possible to not make the effort. God gave me the inspiration to make the effort; he gave me such a mind that I could make the effort.

In our tradition of sanatana dharma or vedic dharma, God has been described as beyond definition. Other races, religions and sects have tried to explain, give a form and definition to God so that you may step on at least the first rung of the ladder that will take you to the roof. It is only to help you that avataras and sages have spoken of Ishwara, Allah, Khuda and God. People have said that God has a form, and also that he is formless, that he lives in Kashi Vishwanath, and that he lives everywhere, is everywhere. This is the statement that Prahlad made to Hiranyakashyapa.

Jale Vishnuh thale Vishnurvishnuh parvatamastake Jwaalaamaalaakule Vishnuh sarvam Vishnumayam jagat.

Vishnu is in the waters, in space, on the mountain tops, in the garland of flames, in every nook and corner of the world.

God lives in Vaikuntha, Kailash, Kashi Vishwanath, the little temple in your house and everywhere else. It has been said that there is nothing other than God, Aham Brahmasmi. Formless was not how God was defined in the beginning. In our tradition, at the beginning God was defined through millions of gods and goddesses: Indra, Varuna, Agni, Surya . . . everything was described as God. There is nothing other than God, and if there is none but God, then who is the other one? There is no one else.

So there is no need to go into these things. Just follow whatever precept is required to live a balanced life. Your house gets cobwebs and dust every day, and you have to clean it. It is the nature of the body to accumulate waste matter, and you have to eliminate it. The biggest obstacle in the way of experiencing the soul is the bondage of illusion, *maya*. Just as the light cannot shine out if there is carbon on the glass of a lantern, in the same way maya holds every person in bondage. If you can free yourself of the bonds, there is no way the light will not shine out. However, we like to keep ourselves tied up so we can call for help if needed. We are all animals tied to poles. It is not possible for an animal that is tied to a pole to graze in the forest even it wants to. It will have to break the bond. The breaking of bonds means expansion of one's energy field. Whether you are a sannyasin or householder, you should stay free of bonds.

I would like to hear more about the importance of fate and purushartha.

Everyone has to do purushartha, exert, whether or not fate exists. The train will arrive at the station at its prescribed time, not earlier. If you reach the station two hours early, you will have to go for a stroll. In the same way, we will get whatever destiny has decided for us. So the question arises, why should we do anything at all?

We have to exert because we cannot exist without action. What will you do if you do not do anything? If you get money, a house and everything else that you wanted, what will you do? People work out of a sense of self, out of their *ahamkara*, ego; they work because life demands work, because work is an inseparable part of life.

Destiny and purushartha are two different things. This is what I have seen in my life. I did not desire whatever I got. I could not even have believed that all this would happen. I spent twelve years in my guru's ashram in Rishikesh, and I used to work very hard there. After that, I became a *bhikshuk*, beggar. I would spread a blanket and put a bowl in front of me at fairs. From whatever money people gave, I would buy my meals and then sleep in a dharmashala. I would keep wandering. I could never have imagined that I would spread yoga to every corner of the world! Yoga is not my subject either, I never studied it. I studied Vedanta and Sanskrit. I have asked myself, "How did all this happen? You did not think or act, you did not have the capability or even the courage." Then I studied the lives of many people and thought about it. I came to the conclusion that whatever one has to receive from destiny, one will receive, and the work that one does is the need of ahamkara, the ego.

If you can stay without action, there is no problem. For as long as I could not stay without work, I worked. Now, for the last several years I have lived without work. I sit the whole day through and it is not a problem. I am comfortable, no thoughts come, no worries come. I do not feel any sense of responsibility, do not get any desires. I just keep on sitting. When a person comes to this state, he can give up work.

Do we achieve artha and kama through prarabdha karma or through purushartha?

Different people have different notions about artha and kama. Some people say that everything is achieved through *prarabdha* (actions of past lives bound to fructify in the present life). They say that if there is grace, we will receive ample. However, from what we see in the world today, from what is obvious, it appears that the basis of wealth is purushartha and industry.

Today, the most developed country in the world is the United States of America, it is the super-power. The second most economically advanced country is Japan. Look at these two countries. What is the behaviour of their people, how do they live, study, bring up their children, look after their parents? What is the law and order situation there? When you look at all these things, then it seems that the basis of wealth is not prarabdha, but purushartha.

What is purushartha or industry? Who is an industrious person? A shopkeeper cannot be called industrious. A farmer who is ploughing the fields cannot be called industrious. A hardworking person is not necessarily industrious. 'Industry' is a complicated word. Many things are included in it. Take life – what is the definition of life? It is not just the motion of the heart and the lungs. In the same way, the definition of industry includes all things from childhood to old age. The biggest example of industry right now is America. The Anglo-Saxon race in particular is very industrious. We do not have the kind of wealth and facilities that they do. The amount that some people earn over their whole lives in India, they earn in a month.

Artha means wealth, and *kama* means wish, not carnal desire. You wish for a family, a man, woman or children. These are different kinds of wishes. When one's wish is not fulfilled, it remains a dream. There are many boys in this village who want to become something, but cannot because the facilities do not exist.

For any person to become big, for progress, it is necessary to have the facilities of an education that is in keeping with the times. In our country education does not keep up with the times. A boy who has received a BA degree does not even know how to write a job application. It is possible to get a job only by coming into contact with the right people. It is not as if people are not talented or worthy of jobs. However, the governing system of our country is such that the education system suffers.

In a country where the governing system is good, the education system will also be good. If you receive a good education, you will get a job. If there are jobs, money will be generated. If money is generated, the market will benefit. If the market is benefited, industries will produce more, and the demand and supply chain will go up. Here, a village woman wears the same sari for six years. There is no demand, because money is necessary for demand. To spend you have to have the ability to earn. To have the ability to earn, you have to have the skill to earn, and for this the right education is necessary. None of this exists. Then why do you speak of prarabdha?

What, after all, is the effect of prarabdha on life?
The word 'prarabdha' is used only for your satisfaction. Make a person drink the alcohol of prarabdha so he can go on saying, "God, only this much was written for me in my fate."

60

This is just mental drunkenness. Not you, but your future generations will have to answer for this.

When I went to Rishikesh, I did not know anything. When Swami Satsangi came to Deoghar, she did not know anything. The university students of today do not know anything. I received all my education at my guru's ashram: civil engineering, electrical engineering, accountancy, banking, prayer and worship, driving, and so on. I received the kind of training that, no matter what conditions you place me in, I can do the work. Make me the managing director of a company and I will run it because I know what management is and how it is executed. It was what I learnt in my guru's ashram that has been of use to me till today. What I studied at school was of no use. What did I learn? The name of Aurangzeb's daughter and how many brothers Ashoka had. Do you get a job with all this? You get a job, artha and kama, through industry.

I am not saying that there is nothing like prarabdha. I believe in the vedic point of view, but to explain everything away through the notion of prarabdha is not what even our ancestors prescribed. Vedanta speaks of sanchita karma, prarabdha karma, agami karma, etc. and explains the principle of *karma*, cause and effect, very well. I am not negating the idea of prarabdha karma, but what I said about the Americans remains true as well. They really did work hard, and the results are visible to everyone.

It has also been said, "First prarabdha was created, then the body. So don't worry too much, just sing God's name."
Where does prarabdha begin? Who is prarabdha's father? The father of prarabdha is karma. And the father of karma is prarabdha. The egg came from the chicken, and the chicken came from the egg. When you understand this, you will find the balance between the two, which is essential.

Without action, there is no cause and without cause there is no action. After all, what was prarabdha born of? Is the egg the cause or the chicken the cause? Is action the cause or

61

prarabdha the cause? The sages say that action is the cause, not prarabdha. Why is action the cause? The upanishads say that first God was one, then He wanted to become many, so He created the whole world. Therefore, the first action was performed by God. The creation of the universe was the first action. The universe is formed of the formless, attributeless Brahman. How did a formless thing assume form? A formless thing assumed form because this was the action performed by God. It is from God that action has come into being, and it is from action that prarabdha has begun.

There has to be prarabdha. If a fruit comes from the mango tree, the seed will follow. When the seed emerges, again the tree will be born, and then fruits, seeds, and so on. The pattern will continue. In the same way, karma arose from God. The father of *adi karma*, first action, is not prarabdha but Param Purusha. From Param Purusha, karma was born. What was that karma? It was the creation of Vishnu, the preserver of creation, and Shiva, the destroyer of creation. From these two karmas, prarabdha was born, gods and goddesses were born, nature was born, maya was born.

Similarly, whichever race worked and acted, they performed karma and received the results of that karma. India was under foreign rule for so many years. Many people

like Mangal Pandey, the queen of Jhansi, Tatya Tope, Dhudhu Pant, etc. worked to free India, but it was only through the effort of Mahatma Gandhi that India became independent. Gandhi was successful because his karma synchronized with India's prarabdha karma. If he, too, had picked up the sword, perhaps he would not have been successful. His arrow of non-violence hit the mark. Through it, the prarabdha karma of India was eliminated.

SANNYASA

Sannyasa is easy; you do not need any education to take sannyasa. In ancient times, in the vedic period, the age for sannyasa was accepted as seventy-five and above. At that age, people would leave their homes and set out for a life of renunciation. Even the kings would follow this dictum. They had seen the world, and *vairagya*, non-attachment, was natural to them, bhakti was natural to them. A person's mind changes at the age of seventy-five. However, this vedic tradition of sannyasa did not last for long, because the fact remains that sannyasa is such a *vritti*, tendency, that it can manifest at any age within a person. It is not necessary to wait till you are seventy-five.

People like Shukadeva and Sanat Kumar were born with the sannyasa instinct. They had the *bhava*, propensity, for sannyasa from the day they were born. There have been many other such great men and women. At the age of eight, Shankaracharya experienced the sannyasa bhava. Lord Buddha experienced it at the age of thirty-six. Lord Mahavira ran away from the altar at his wedding to take sannyasa. Therefore, the thinkers in society advocated that the tradition of sannyasa be open to everyone.

The first condition

When someone takes sannyasa at a young age, however, they have to deal with many things which one does not need to deal with during old age. For example, I no longer need to deal with desire or attachment, but if a boy or girl of ten, fifteen or eighteen comes to sannyasa, there is much they have to unravel. Towards this end, all ashrams from the times of Buddha, Mahavira and Shankaracharya have ruled that the first condition of sannyasa is to cut off all bonds. If you can cut the bonds of the mind and the body, the external and internal bonds, then come to sannyasa life. If you cannot, then do not come. This is the first rule.

When a young boy or girl comes to the sannyasa ashram, they are not taught asana, pranayama, dharana, dhyana and the *Bhagavad Gita* to begin with. The first thing they learn is to cut off bonds. After accepting sannyasa, one no longer has any connection with family, race or religion, whether external or internal. One is pure, satchidananda spirit, not the body. Such a person, who can free the spirit from the bonds of society and desires, may take to sannyasa life. This is the first condition, and it eliminates 99.99 percent of people, in the same way that a sieve separates chaff from flour.

You want to take sannyasa and also say to your father, "Father, I am well. These days I look after the accounts office." It does not work. Sannyasa is not a job; in a sense, it is suicide. Until such time that you cut off your head, you will not get a new head. If you want to save your old ways and also take sannyasa, you will have neither, everything will finish. If you want sannyasa, you will have to get rid of the old mind.

In the first step of sannyasa, this elimination takes place. After that, the aspirants stay in an ashram and help to run it. In some ashrams people are fed the whole day through. All sannyasins join in this activity and they do the same work the whole day through. In Rishikesh there are many such ashrams; they run hospitals, schools, Sanskrit classes, and so on. The Swaminarayan sect in Gujarat runs colleges. Sannyasins are able to perform the varied duties well because all their ties have been cut off. Their mind is now at one place; they do not call their parents. This is not enforced either. The bonds of the world, maya and mind cannot be cut off forcefully. A light awakens and one realizes, "I am Swami

Satyananda." Who is Swami Satyananda? This body is not Swami Satyananda, it will go to the grave. Who then is Swami Satyananda? Who am I?

Material life and sannyasa life

Sannyasins realize that they cannot evolve by living in the world. One may earn money by living in the world, enjoy the company of the opposite sex, satisfy desires, look after one's comfort, but one cannot know oneself. If someone wants to know himself while living in the world, he will have to be a very special person, like King Janaka or Ramakrishna Paramahamsa. Not everyone can do this.

It is possible to realize God while living a material life, but for most people this is a principle, not the reality. If your mind is running after wife, children, promotion and legal cases, which mind will you give to God? You have only one mind. If you had two minds, this would have worked – one mind in the world, the other with God. Surdas has written:

Udho man naahin dasa-beesa
Eka huto so gayo Shyaama sanga kaun araadhai eesa.

(The gopis say) O Uddhava, we do not possess ten or twenty minds. The only mind we had has gone with Shyama (Krishna), who now should worship the absolute God (that you speak of)?

There is only one mind, whether you focus it on God or in the world.

What you can do while living in the world, however, is to prepare for the day when vairagya awakens in you and you have perception of God. Most people get married at twenty-five, retire at sixty, and then travel about or do similar things. Where is God in your life? To realize God you do not have to do anything, you only have to know yourself. God is within. This is the truth; know just this much. Idol worship, visiting temples, prayer, worship, etc. are fine. They have to be done to appease the mind, because our religions prescribe them.

65

But God is within. It has been said:

Sarva niwaasee sadaa alepaa tuhe sanga samaaee
Puhupa madhya jyon vaasa vasata hai,
mukura madhya jasa chhaaee
Vaise hee Hari vasai nirantara,
ghatahi khojahu bhaaee.

He lives everywhere. He remains untouched by all. He permeates you. Just as fragrance dwells in the flower and the image in the mirror, the Lord lives within you eternally. Search for him within your own self.

God is verily within me, and God is also outside me.

Jita dekhoon, tita Rama

Wherever I look, there is Rama

The essence of God is subtle, and it is beyond the scope of the senses, mind, dream, wakefulness or death. That effulgent God is within us. Grihastha ashrama is the preparation for this realization, and sannyasa ashrama is its postgraduate stage. Therefore, nothing remains in sannyasa ashrama. What happens in our ashram? We make buildings, prepare food, teach the kanyas, that's all. But when a sannyasin performs a task, he must do it with the feeling that he is serving the Almighty. The feeling that one is an accountant or an in-charge should not be there.

The freedom of sannyasa

There are many traditions of sannyasa in India. Among them the Dashnami tradition to which we belong is very strong. Dashnami sannyasins live freely and independently. We do not take the government's help, we are not dependent on its monetary help or support. We build our own life. A sannyasin must always remain self-reliant.

Besides Dashnami, there is the Vaishnava tradition. Vaishnavas are largely found in Puri, Ayodhya and Mathura. They are called sadhus. The third sannyasa tradition is Udasi, founded by Guru Nanak's son, Srichandra. There is another sect of Brahma Kumaris. They are a very strong and honest people, not hollow. In this way, many are working for the cause of sannyasa.

All the sects of sannyasins in India live like a donkey without its owner. No one controls them. They do not live in ashrams by profession. What kind of a sannyasin is he who is controlled by someone? Such a person cannot be a sannyasin. A sannyasin controls himself. He must decide for himself whether or not he wants to drink poison, smoke, have attachments. Society cannot tell a sannyasin what he should or should not do. He must decide for himself, only then is he a sannyasin.

Sannyasa is a very big tradition of this country and it will remain that way because it is not dependent on the support of the government. Sannyasins do not live to please or be pleased by anyone. We do not want anything from anyone. We are not a religious sect, we are not interested in spreading religion. I used to visit so many different countries, but I did not convert anyone to Hinduism. Why should you change someone's religion?

A sannyasin should remain completely independent. If he does not like it somewhere, he should be able to just pick up his bags and leave. Kabir has said,

> *Mana laago mero yaara phakeeree men*
> *Jo sukha paavon Raama bhajana men,*
> *so sukha naahin ameeree men*
> *Premanagara men rahani hamaaree,*
> *bhalee bani aaee sabooree men*
> *Haatha men kundee bagala men sota,*
> *chaaro disi jaageeree men*
> *Aakhira tana yaha khaaka milega,*
> *kahan phirata magarooree men.*

My mind is engrossed in the life of a recluse. The pleasure that lies in the chanting of the Lord's name does not lie in riches. Listen patiently to all that people say, the good and the bad, and live a life of simplicity. I live in the city of love, my contentment gives me happiness. All I possess is a yoga danda and a water pot, and I move about everywhere. This body will become one with ashes, why then do you assume pride?

Whether a sannyasin lives in a palace or hut, he should live like a recluse. You might have read the life stories of Ramakrishna Paramahamsa, Swami Vivekananda and Anandamai Ma. There have been many others like them. My guru, Swami Sivananda, was a great doctor, and even after establishing such a large ashram, he lived simply. There are many examples of such ideal sannyasins.

GURU MANTRA

All spiritual aspirants must keep two things in mind. First, they must practise asana regularly for at least fifteen minutes every day. The aged, too, should practise asana without fail. I am over eighty years of age, but I practise asana for fifteen minutes every day. Second, never forget to do at least five minute's japa of your guru mantra every morning and evening with a one-pointed mind. I have not said fifteen minutes, just five minutes. The practice of japa should not be done as and when you wish. The mantra has come from the guru, not from your own mind. A guru is necessary for attainment of any knowledge, and a guru is necessary also to attain knowledge of yoga.

Before practising japa, you should resolve that during the practice you will not think of the world, but remain one-pointed. It is important to realize that mantra is not only necessary, it is the foundation, the basis for making the mind one-pointed. To be able to make the mind one-pointed means acquiring the master key of life in your hands. If you want to control the destiny of your life, the only way is to learn the art of concentration. It does not matter whether one is a thief or a crook, a saint or a sage, young or old, pious, celibate or immoral. One whose mind enters the state of void acquires the key.

Three states of void

Entering the void, *shoonya*, means a state where there is no worldly awareness. This state of void has to be attained three times, not just once. What I am telling you about is the state of the first void. *Om namah Shivaya*, nothing else in the mind – this is the state of the first void.

Kabir says that the supreme state that you want to attain is beyond the three states of void – *shoonya, shoonya, shoonya ke par*. He said, *Jagrat, swapna, sushupti jani, turiya tar milaya*. "It was when I realized the conscious, the dream and the deep sleep states that I tuned into the super-conscious state." *Jagrat*, wakeful or conscious, is the first state of void. Attain the first state of void in the awakened state, the second state of void in *swapna*, the dream state, and the third state of void in *sushupti*, the deep sleep state. Thereafter, the fourth state, *turiya*, will arrive.

The unseen reality

I will try to explain this in a different way. The state which you are in at present, where the eyes are open, the mind is functioning, and there is a relationship between the mind and the sense organs, is known as the conscious or wakeful state. From the five sense organs – ears, skin, eyes, tongue and nose – develop five perceptions – sound, touch, form, taste and smell. As long as you are aware of these five perceptions, that state is known as the jagrat state. In this state it is necessary to completely cut off the relationship with the sense perceptions for a few moments. Five minutes are enough. If the bullet hits the target, then just one bullet is enough. If for one moment you enter the state of void, miracles will happen. For within rests the supreme soul. Kabir has said:

In this pitcher seven oceans exist,
Some are sweet, some are salty.
In this pitcher a million jewels exist,
Some are emeralds, some are diamonds.
In this pitcher the creator exists.

70

The creator cannot be seen. A doctor may cut you up, but he will not be able to see the creator or the seven seas. The marrow, bones and blood are visible. But the poet says that within this vessel, the body, exist nine million gems. There are seven seas within this vessel, some sweet and some salty. Within this vessel exists the creator. But you see nothing within. You only see blinding darkness. Now the question is, why can't you see anything?

You cannot see because you do not have the eyes. Without eyes, you cannot see an object, without the intellect you cannot see thoughts, without a microscope you cannot see bacteria. You cannot see nuclear radiation with your eyes or even with a microscope. Its sensor is different. To know any object, you need the right sensor. The sensor catches radio waves, laser rays and nuclear radiation, the things that cannot be seen. So, if an object cannot be seen, it does not mean that it does not exist. If an object cannot be seen, but all the saints and sages have said that it exists, and you say it does not, it is because you do not have the eyes to see it. To open those eyes, one-pointedness is the key, the path. It is through the path of concentration that you can go in. There is no other way. The temple, mosque, church, *Bible*, *Bhagavad Gita* or *Ramayana* are not the path. There is only one way: for just one moment try to become one-pointed.

Limits of japa

Do not try to concentrate the mind for too long. I am giving you a warning, a danger signal. Those who try to concentrate their minds for too long, for an hour or an hour and a half, begin to get depressed. You might have noticed that the students who score the highest always appear to be self-absorbed, for the level of concentration of the student who is very bright is very high. Therefore, to become one-pointed, do your guru mantra for only five minutes. Do not try to meditate or concentrate at any time of the day. Do not assume the posture of padmasana at whim!

If you have a guru mantra, then the first thing to do is to start japa regularly and one-pointedly. Enjoy yourself the whole day long, do whatever you wish to, but resolve in your head that from today you will find five minutes at night for japa, no matter how much work you have or the troubles you are in. After all, you go to the toilet no matter what, so do this as well.

The day my guru gave me the mantra, he said, "Five malas in the morning and five malas in the evening." I said to him, "Only five malas?" He said, "Yes." I said, "Shouldn't this be increased?" He replied, "Do you go on increasing the amount you eat every day? There is a rule for meals. If you do three malas today, and the next month ten, then twenty-five and then forty, you will get indigestion. Believe in this." I said, "Swamiji, how then will I evolve?" He said, "If one who knows how to hit the target shoots just one bullet, it is enough. One who does not know how to hit the target may shoot a hundred bullets, but no one will die. What will you do by repeating ten malas?"

My guru asked me to do five malas, but later I realized how difficult that is. I would sit, and after one mala my mind would be lost. The mala would drop from my hands; I would not even know whether I had crossed the sumeru. If you have ever experienced this, if you ever experience it, then you will know what I am talking about. I do not remember if I ever completed five malas. It would fall, I would pick it up again, and then wonder where to begin. So I would begin from the beginning. The mala would again fall. When the mind becomes one-pointed, the connection with the senses is cut off. The fingers uncurl by themselves and the mala falls down. This is true, try concentrating and see. In that moment, there is only you, nothing else.

Now I am old, but I still do only five malas. I do not want to exceed this number, because Guruji used to say that if you do five malas properly, then even five malas are not necessary. If you do only one mala properly, even one mala is not necessary. If you believe that it is right to remain occupied in

72

the objects of the world, then for one minute believe that it is wrong. For one minute remove your mind from the world so that instead of shooting a hundred arrows, you shoot only one; but shoot like a sharpshooter who pierces his target. One mala is enough. This is what happened in my life. Once I sat in padmasana, and the mala fell. I did not even realize that it had fallen. I relate this experience often. It must have been eight or nine in the evening. When I came to, it was four in the morning. I felt very happy, I thought I had attained samadhi. For eight hours I was sitting in padmasana, the body did not move, the mind did not move, and the mala fell – a matter of great joy. So I sent a note to Swamiji describing the incident. Swamiji said, "Samadhi is not child's play. *Bar bar muni jatan haranhi, anta Rama kahin avata nahin*: Again and again the sage tries, but at the end of his life the Lord still does not come. After working for many lifetimes, finally the soul finds the supreme path. You say you achieved this in a night! You had fallen asleep, my son." He said this and I believed him.

Fruits of concentration

The one-pointedness that I am talking about affects one at three places. The first effect is on the entire functioning of the body. The effects of concentration have been observed on the enzymes, hormones, DNA, the heart, lungs, brain, and so on. Read our books, they clearly state what kind of changes come about in the body through the practice of concentration. Second, it influences the receptivity and response levels of a person. Your responses and receptivity become sharper. Third, your capability to perform is enhanced.

For five minutes, repeat the same mantra, that's all. When you achieve this one-pointedness, then you will find the way to go in. And when you find the way to go in, your capacity to work and your responses will improve, whether in studies or elsewhere. There have been many great musicians and artists in the world. Michelangelo, for example. What an incredible work he did at the Vatican! He would climb up in the morning with a bottle of water, lie flat on the scaffolding, and go on painting the ceiling till evening. This is not normal, it is exceptional. Not only the spiritual path, but every path requires dedication. But spirituality is such a path that if you walk it, you can become a very good musician, sportsperson, yogi, ruler, poet, writer, politician, and a crook too.

Swami Vivekananda's achievements were remarkable. He lived for only thirty-two years. Until he was eighteen, he was studying. So he had only ten or twelve years to work, but he performed a miracle. He could do this because his actions were of a very high level, his thoughts were solid and his plans were accurate. Another person born eighteen or nineteen hundred years before Swami Vivekananda also displayed exceptional calibre. This was Adi Shankaracharya. At the age of eight, he took sannyasa. Similarly, Swami Niranjan came to me at the age of four to take sannyasa and went abroad at the age of ten. This is unusual.

After taking sannyasa, Adi Shankaracharya came to the banks of the Narmada. He took initiation from Govindapada and stayed with him for a while. Then he went to Vyas Chatti, where he wrote commentaries on the *Bhagavad Gita*, the *Brahma Sutras* and upanishads, which are considered high literature all over the world today. Shankaracharya was able to do this because he was filled to the brim with spiritual consciousness. At eight Shankaracharya left home, at twenty-two he awakened the vedic dharma across the length and breadth of the country, and at thirty he died.

Go within

To make the mind one-pointed, the guru mantra is the foundation. Religion, rituals, behaviour or thinking are of no consequence. Go on doing japa for a year, two years, ten years . . . after all, it takes fifteen years to become an MBBS, and a similar amount of time to accomplish other sciences. If the doors open for you in fifteen or twenty years, consider it a wonderful thing. The mantra is the key to open the door. Learn how to go within with the mantra.

74

It is very difficult to go in. When you go within at night in your dreams, can you control your dreams? When you cannot control your thoughts, how will you control your dreams? When you cannot control your gross mind, how will you control your subtle mind? When you do not have control over your gross body, *sthoola sharira*, how then will you control your subtle body, *sukshma sharira*? And if you do not have control over your subtle body, how will you control your causal body, *karana sharira*? The causal body wakes up in the deep sleep state, the state of *nidra*. In the dream state, you experience the subtle body. In the state of wakefulness, you experience the gross body.

There are three bodies – gross, subtle and causal. The states of *jagrat*, *swapna* and *sushupti* are connected with the gross, subtle and causal bodies. In the state of deep sleep, the individual goes into the causal body. However, you do not have control over sleep, or dreaming, or anger. You should not get angry, but you do. There is no control, just as a lame person knows that stairs can be climbed, but he cannot climb them. He knows that it is possible to run, but he cannot do it. We know that anger can be controlled, but we cannot do it. We do not have control over any of the modifications of the mind. So I have placed all these things in front of you. Don't try too many different things, just hold on to a small thing and walk on.

75

BALANCING THE OPPOSITES

When you are pursuing pleasure, you experience imbalances in life. The pursuit of sensory objects is the pursuit of pleasure, *bhoga*. This happens to you every day, 365 days a year, throughout your life the association of the senses with sense objects remains established. When this association persists, negative factors influence the psychological body so that you are subject to diseases.

Life is full of happiness and unhappiness, and changes come about in the human body with the onset of these states. The cardiogram, the brain waves and the blood pressure all display changes depending on your state of joy and sorrow. However, if you practise yoga, balance is attained.

It is not possible to withdraw from the world of senses. You have to stay within their influence, it is your compulsion, you are helpless against them. Every one of us has to stay in this world of happiness, unhappiness, passion, anger, envy and delusion. This is the nature of Prakriti. Death is a reality and life is a reality too. It is impossible to experience total fulfilment in this lifetime. That is not the nature of Prakriti. If you were to experience nothing but happiness from birth to death, you would go mad. Unhappiness comes to balance out happiness, and happiness comes to balance out unhappiness. Just as the day dawns to balance out the night and the night sets in to balance out the day, in the same way you need yoga to smooth out the imbalances created in the body due to the pursuit of pleasure.

In the state of society today, we complain about everything all the time, whether in newspapers, television or our conversations. No one is happy with anything. This is how life is perceived. However, your perception of life should be such that you develop a sattwic state of mind. This is necessary not just for the individual, but for the society, the family and the nation. If, with the practice of yoga, you are able to change the direction of your mind, it is possible that a positive thinking pattern will emerge from within.

MAKAR SANKRANTI

Makar Sankranti is celebrated on 14th January all over India. In some places it is called Khichari Sankranti, in some Til Sankranti, at others Pongal. In South India it is called Pongal, and *pongal* means khichari. On this day in Kerala, people gather together at temples, set up stoves and cooking vessels and prepare pongal. There are prayers and the traditional five instruments, drum, veena, etc., are played. Caparisoned elephants are walked down the streets. After preparing the khichari, everyone takes it back home in their respective cooking vessels.

Makar Sankranti is also celebrated in Sri Lanka, Kashmir, Uttaranchal, Kumaon and Garhwal. This is India's biggest festival based on the solar calendar. All other festivals are based on the lunar calendar, whether Shivaratri, Janmashtami or Navaratri. Makar Sankranti is the only festival based on the solar calendar, because it is the day when the sun stops in the house of Capricorn and turns back towards the house of Cancer. Now the days start getting longer and the nights shorter.

Makar Sankranti is in fact associated with several traditions. One is the eating of khichari, curd and rice flakes. The second is the ritual of bathing in the Ganga. The third is the association with the sun and astronomy, and the fourth is the association with yoga.

The descent of Ganga

The river Ganga originates at the Gomukh glacier in the Himalayas. From Gomukh, it descends to Gangotri. A temple dedicated to Mother Ganga exists there. Nearby is the rock of Bhagirath. At this spot, King Bhagirath is believed to have done penance so that Ganga would descend down to earth from the heavens. It is a famous story.

Kapil Muni had cursed the seven thousand sons of King Sagar to die by fire. In order to liberate their souls, Ganga had to be brought down from the heavens. Several kings attempted this, but in vain. At the end, Bhagirath, king of *Ikshvaku* (an eminent solar dynasty) succeeded. The rock near Gangotri is attributed to him. Higher up, about twenty kilometres from there, is the Gomukh glacier. From there, the Ganga flows down to the plains, towards Prayagraj, through Varanasi, Munger and Kolkata before reaching Ganga Sagar. Ganga Sagar is a tiny island, and here the river meets with the sea. *Gangasagar* means the meeting of Ganga and the sea. On that island there is a temple dedicated to Kapil Muni. On Makar Sankranti, a big fair is held at Ganga Sagar, and from here to Gangotri, all along the banks of the Ganga, thousands of people bathe in the river.

Two paths of yoga

The association of Makar Sankranti with yoga is esoteric. In yoga they say that on this day the sun ascends – is in uttarayana, and on Karka Sankranti, the sun descends – is in dakshinayana. These are the two paths: northwards or *uttarayana*, and southwards or *dakshinayana*.

Those who want to understand yoga should know that uttarayana and dakshinayana are the two paths an aspirant can walk on. The *jivatma*, individual soul, that practises yoga, travels on one of these paths. One soul may go the uttarayana route, and another the dakshinayana route. The experience of these paths takes place in the state of dhyana in this living body.

There are two asanas for dhyana: padmasana and siddhasana. You cannot practise dhyana sitting in an armchair because to achieve dhyana you need to do mudra, bandha, asana and pranayama. When you practise dhyana, what happens? In the state of dhyana, your mind exists in one of the five states. The mind may run here and there, be in a state of depression, excitement, restlessness, sleep or one-pointedness. In yoga, these states are called *moodha*, dull, *kshipta*, scattered, *vikshipta*, oscillating between dissipation and one-pointedness, *ekagra*, one-pointed, and *nirodha*, cessation. The mind stays at one point or the other, on some movement or the other, it moves from place to place and stays in some state or the other. Does it or not? The mind fixes itself on something or the other. The mind has two important moods – uttarayana and dakshinayana.

The *Bhagavad Gita* (8:24–26) refers to the paths of uttarayana and dakshinayana:

Agnirjyotirahah shuklah shanmaasaa uttaraayanam
Tatra prayaataa gacchanti brahma brahmavido janaah.

Fire, light, daytime, the bright fortnight, the six months of the northern path of the sun, departing by these, those who know Brahman go to Brahman.

This is the reference to uttarayana. Dakshinayana has been referred to as:

Dhoomo raatristathaa krishnah shanmaasaa dakshinaayanam
Tatra chaandramasam jyotiryogee praapya nivartate.

Attaining the lunar light by smoke, night time, the dark fortnight, also the six months of the southern path of the sun, the yogi returns.

Then it is said:

Shuklakrishne gatee hyete jagatah shaashvate mate
Ekayaa yaatyanaavrittimanyayaa'vartate punah.

The bright and the dark paths of the world are verily thought to be eternal; by the one (the bright path) one goes not to return and by the other (the dark path) one returns.

In travelling on one path, the yogi does not return. If he travels on the other path, it is possible that he will come and go. For spiritual aspirants, Makar Sankranti represents the path of uttarayana. What is uttarayana? Who goes on this path? And who goes on the path of dakshinayana?

79

Nada, bindu, kala

From nada, bindu and kala three forms emerge. *Nada* means sound. I am talking now. Does the sound of my voice have a form? Does my nada have a form? It does, but you cannot see it with your eyes. However, you can see the form of a *bindu*, point. I am a point. In a temple, Shiva is a point. Guru is a point. These are all points. What is *kala?* The experience that arises within your mind is called kala. Nada, bindu and kala: sound, object of concentration and internal experience are the three essential forms. The one who holds on to these three forms while walking the path of dhyana, yoga, spirituality and dharma is said to have taken the uttarayana route. The one walking the uttarayana path always sees the light within. He sees the inner light.

In the vedic literature, *Paramatma*, the supreme spirit, is considered to be without form. He is considered formless, imperceptible, *trikalateet*, beyond time, *shabadateet*, beyond description. He is faceless. He does not have a place or name, but for the purpose of sadhana, that formless God has been given a form. The form is imagined. Never make a mistake on this point. The sadhana which is done on a form is the way to experience sadhana on the formless.

Chakras

From mooladhara chakra to anahata chakra is the dakshinayana path. From anahata chakra to ajna chakra is the uttarayana path. If kundalini reaches anahata chakra, then it has reached the point of no return. If it reaches up to manipura chakra, it can return or descend at any time. *Swapishi kulakunde kuharini* (*Saundarya Lahari* v.10) – it can descend to its resting place and go to sleep. The resting place of kundalini is swadhisthana. The word *swadhishthana* means your own residence. So kundalini goes back to its residence and falls asleep. After reaching anahata chakra, however, kundalini is unobstructed, unhindered. Thereafter, it does not return. *Anavrittim, anavrittim* – no return, no retreat.

80

After anahata, there is vishuddhi chakra, and after vishuddhi, ajna chakra. The Ganga flows till here. Beyond this, there is no Ganga; beyond this lies the sea. That very Ganga becomes the sea. The sages have sung,

Muralee kaun bajaave gagan mandal ke beech?
Gangaa-Jamunaa beech muralee baaje,
uttar dishee dhuni hove
Vahan muralee kee teraee suni-suni rahe gopikaa moha
Muralee kaun bajaave?

Who plays the flute in the centre of the skies? The flute plays between Ganga and Yamuna, in the northern realm. There, hearing the music of the flute, the gopis are enraptured. Who plays the flute?

Between Ganga and Yamuna, the flute plays at ajna chakra. The ajna chakra is your Prayagraj, where Ganga, Yamuna and Saraswati meet. It is *Triveni Sangam*, the meeting point. Right behind the eyebrow centre in the medulla oblongata is the position of ajna chakra. There Ganga, Yamuna and Saraswati meet. After that, Gangasagar begins. Those who travel on the uttarayana path travel from anahata chakra. Those who travel on the dakshinayana path start from mooladhara.

Man is different from other species because of his ability to have *yoga*, union. All other human faculties are also present in animals. Whatever you do, animals can do as well. It has been said:

Aahaara nidraa bhaya maithunam
cha samaanam etat pashubhih naraanaam.
Jnanam naraanaamadhiko vishesho
jnanena heenaah pashubhih samaanaah.

The basic instincts of hunger, sleep, fear and procreation are common to human beings and animals. It is knowledge alone that distinguishes man from animal.

81

Man has only one special quality that separates him from animals, and that is yoga. *Yoga* means the ability to go within and to be able to turn the mind towards the uttarayana path. This is reiterated in our dharma, our traditions and the instructions given to us by our gurus. I am not saying anything new. I am only giving you a small reminder.

MARRIAGE

If you are married, it is better to stick together until it becomes impossible to do so. If your clothes get torn, you stitch them back together. They get torn again, and again you stitch up the torn part. You could continue to repair a dress for as long as possible. However, if you are extravagant, you will throw it away and buy another one. The relationship between a man and woman, husband and wife, should not be based on extravagance. In English it is said that marriage is made in heaven and conducted in church. In India we say that for seven lives we will not leave each other.

I feel that marriage is the only relationship that has endured excellence in history. A man and woman who are total strangers promise to overcome that strangeness and merge into each other physically, mentally and spiritually. This is a promise between two strangers. All other relationships are a familiar part of life, whether father and daughter, brother and sister, etc. A husband and wife are total strangers, they have nothing in common. If you have a brother, you have no choice but to have him as your brother. If you are a daughter, you have no choice but to be the daughter. But when you want to pick up a stranger, you have a choice. Yes? So, that 'yes' has to be a permanent 'yes'.

As far as difficulties in relationships are concerned, they are mostly due to lack of sensual gratification. You can manage that sensuality through spiritual life. Explore music, art, painting, anything. In India, a husband and wife could not divorce each other until 1962. Now the law has changed, but even then divorce is not the first option. If there are problems, the wife will go back to her parents' house for a while, but she will return. She will go away again and return again. He, too, will return to her.

The important thing, in my opinion, is not the gratification of sensuality. You are alone, incomplete, and when somebody comes into your life, you become complete. So, a complete equation has to be created. What is the essence behind this? Purusha and Prakriti. The man represents spirit and the woman represents matter. Spirit and matter come together and then there is totality, oneness. So, difficulties should be treated with patience, wisdom and endurance. You have to find a way out until you know there is no solution at all.

There are two aspects to married life. In ancient days you married because you needed progeny. Progeny between people of the same genetic code, such as brother and sister, was not favourable. One had to find a partner of another genetic code so that the progeny did not suffer from genetic diseases, etc. Here emotion did not play much of a part. Marriage was a social aspect of life, and this continued for many thousands of years. With the rise of the women's liberation movement, the basis of that fusion became personal attraction, emotion, friendship, etc. However, the social aspects of marriage are enduring; the emotional aspects fade away like colour. So, one has to decide upon the basis of marriage.

FUTURE OF YOGA

Mind's mechanic

When you have a car, you need fuel to run it. However, fuel itself is not enough; you also need a mechanic to repair it from time to time. Similarly, the body needs a mechanic. The various parts of the human mind need a mechanic. If you don't find a mechanic for your mind, mental disaster will follow. However, if you do find a good mechanic, you will feel peaceful, there will be *shanti*. Yoga will play the role of such a mechanic in the years to come.

We are coming to a point where economic problems have been taken care of, and many other problems that our ancestors had do not exist any more. We are living in the age of comfort, affluence, possibility and freedom. When all these things are achieved, the mind becomes free like the devil. In ancient days, to buy a small thing you had to walk for half an hour to the market. To go from Paris to another European country you rode a horse. Now you can reach India from France in five hours. So the mind has very few material problems now. And when the mind has few material problems, it creates psychological problems. That is what the West as well as the East – India, China and all the countries that are now developing – will face.

Yoga has a great promise to keep. The stalwarts who know about the mind and body should devote a lot of time to thinking about yoga in relation to the body and mind. I am not talking about the spirit. That may come after two hundred years perhaps. It came in India once upon a time when everybody became mad about enquiring after the spirit. During Buddha's time, everybody was searching for the soul and spirit. Food, bed, money were not considered necessary, one's self was the only concern. That time will soon come again when most people, especially young people, in the developed countries will say, "Who am I? Where have I come from? What is the cause? What is my ultimate form?" However, to delve into all this will be the last mission of yoga, not its first mission. The first mission of yoga is the body and mind.

Comeback of religion
Religion will again make a comeback. It keeps coming back. It is a cycle. There is a time when you want religion. There is a time when you hate religion. There is a time when you terminate religion. There is a time when you understand religion. There is a time when you do not talk about religion.

All this is cyclic. Religion will come back because religion was born before man was born. The basis of religion is not intellect, but faith.

Everyone carries faith within. Everyone uses faith. If they do not believe in God, they apply their faith elsewhere, such as secularism, a figure like Mahatma Gandhi, and so on. Faith and belief are the basic things that endure until the end of man's life. After all, who has seen God? But God has lived with man from the first day to the last. You may say that you do not believe in God, but just sit down and think, and a point will come when you will say, "How can I deny God when I don't really know him?" You can deny someone you have seen; you cannot deny the one you have not seen. So, faith and belief are the basis of religion.

Nobody can make you religious. The word 'religion' is made of two root words. 'Re' means again and 'legion' means connection. So religion means 'second connection'. We had separated; you were lost in France, I was lost in India for many years, and finally one day we met in Tibet. That is called re-union, religion, meeting again, uniting again. With whom are you going to unite? You were with God, but you got lost and today you are with Mammon. Mammon is material life, indulgence, desires, passions and all that. You did not remember, you did not even think of God.

Close your eyes and look within, and you will see that God is in you. My God is in me. Her God is in her. But it is not as if there are as many Gods as there are people. There are not six billion Gods. God is only one, but He exists separately in six billion people. Six billion bulbs and only one power house! In science we call this the unified field theory. It says that everything is present everywhere. You are all-pervading. I am all-pervading. She is all-pervading. That is the unified field theory.

OPEN-HEART SURGERY

When your arteries are blocked, you become selfish. When your arteries are open, when open-heart surgery has been performed on you, you become selfless. The villagers will be receiving prasad for two months, from now till 14th January, Makar Sankranti. This could only happen because I have been successful in performing open-heart surgery on many of you, and I want to perform more heart surgeries on those whose arteries are blocked.

If you have blocked arteries, open up your heart to me. Do you agree? When your arteries are blocked, you are selfish. When the surgeon opens your heart up, for some time he puts you on an artificial respiratory system. Right now, for these five days, you are all functioning through an artificial heart. Afterwards, you will be back on your normal heart, but with a bypass having been performed by the expert heart surgeon, Swami Satyananda Saraswati. I hope all of you get my message. Remember to think, "Yes, I have a heart block." When your heart is blocked, your cheque remains in the inner pocket.

Those among you who have given generously for the villagers do not have any heart problems because I have been very successful in performing your bypass surgeries.

Be careful that you do not have heart problems! Heart problems do not only take place in the physical body, but also in the mental, spiritual and psychic bodies. These heart problems are more real, and it is on account of these that you are unhappy, dissatisfied, angry or melancholy. So allow me to perform the heart surgery. Will you?

SEA OF SERENITY

I can give you some news. One acre of land has been bought on the moon. It is located on the shore of the Sea of Serenity. The ashram, the yoga movement, has bought a piece of land on the moon. I don't think that many of you believe it. It is a regular deed of sale. The money has been paid, the receipt obtained and the title deed will soon follow.

The moon has been completely mapped. Different points have been given names, so our land is located on the Sea of Serenity. There is no water or air there. There is no atmosphere, but that's the name, Sea of Serenity. By buying land on the moon, I am not shooting in the dark. Several American presidents, too, have bought land there.

The calculation of time in India is related to the moon. The moon is the ruler of time in India, not the sun. We follow a lunar calendar. For example, today is the second day of the bright fortnight of Marga Shirsha, Agrahan. We are talking about the position of the moon, not that of the sun. The moon holds a very important place in the Hindu psyche. Muslims also follow a lunar calendar. They call it *Jantri*, we call it *Panchang*. All their important occasions like Ramazan and Id are dependent on the moon. In fact, their religious symbol is also the moon, the crescent moon.

There is no gravity on the moon. So the moment you go there, your kundalini will shoot up, reach sahasrara and meet Shiva. Yoga will take place. When you come back to the ashram, you will have an awakened kundalini. For that, ten thousand dollars is nothing. So be ready, keep the money in the bank. All yoga ashrams may soon buy small pieces of land, enough for a tent on the moon. Maybe in time the prices will come down!

When you are on the moon, you will not need to do bhastrika pranayama, tadan kriya, intense meditation, controlling the mind and senses to raise the kundalini. You will have to do nothing because kundalini is always eager to go to Shiva. The natural attraction of Shakti is towards Shiva. But the problem is gravity; she can't rise because of gravity. This earth's gravity is maya. Maya is what science calls gravity. Maya does not allow the jiva to get rid of body and mind consciousness. It is always attached to matter; it cannot get out of matter.

The abode of kundalini is swadhisthana, not mooladhara. It has fallen from swadhisthana to mooladhara. Just as you lose your path and are brought back home, in the same way the original abode of kundalini is swadhisthana, the chakra in the tailbone region. From mooladhara, in the coccyx region, you have to bring it back to swadhisthana. This is very difficult. There are hundreds of ways that have been discovered by sages from time to time, which eventually became codified as religion. However, if you go to the moon, do sadhana for a day, just sit in padmasana, close your eyes and chant Om or some other mantra, kundalini will automatically rise.

DEVI

"I have no nationality, I have no religion, I have no gender, I have no language." These are the words of Devi, they form the definition of Devi. Devi has no religion, gender, nationality or language. Perhaps she does not understand English, or Sanskrit or Hindi. She understands only one language, the language of the heart.

All of us are worshippers. Mother is Divine, she is formless. The kanyas and batuks are the medium of Devi, just as wire is the medium of electricity. A wire can be a good or bad conductor. The kanyas and batuks are good conductors of divine energy. For these five days of the yajna, we treat them with full respect. On the fifth day, we will worship and feed them, and ask Devi to bless us through them, for they are the medium. They are not our guests; you and I are the guests. Devi is *nirakara*, formless, and she is also *sakara*, with form, she is Bhagavati.

The worship of Devi in Christianity is known as Novena worship. They worship the goddess for nine days just as we worship Devi for nine days, Navadurga, in the months of Ashwin and Chaitra. Christians have the same custom as us. During the Novena worship, the offering is bread and wine. We don't use bread and wine, we give something more practical, useful and down-to-earth, like rice, oil, soap and salt. This is the prasad.

KANYAS AND BATUKS

The children here are down-to-earth, they are practical. They do not know how to get tired, they have no concept of fatigue and exhaustion. They are very brilliant, very intelligent. Their parents are not here as they work in Deoghar, Asansol, Dhanbad, etc. Only the mothers and grandmothers live here and look after the children. The children say the ashram is their first home. They go to their houses only at night.

All the children come to class here every day. They have English, yoga, kirtan, *Bhagavad Gita*, *Ramayana* and computer classes. We have a very good computer section. This year a hundred kanyas will learn computers. People say, what is the point of their learning computers if they have to get married and collect cow-dung in the morning? I say, even educated people can collect cow-dung. In the villages of European countries there are educated people who live the life of a farmer.

89

FIRE

Before fire was discovered, we had nothing. We used to eat raw fruits, seeds, roots, grains, even raw meat like animals. Suddenly man stumbled upon fire and from then on he maintained the fire. Therefore, the first verse of the *Rig Veda*, the most ancient literature of the world, says,

> *Agnim ile purohitam yajnasya devam*
> *ritvijam hotaram ratnadhatamam.*

We worship the adorable Fire, the chief priest of the yajna. He gets the yajna done in due season. He, as the summoner, is capable of bringing the gods to the yajna performed here.

The first expression of the *Rig Veda* is dedicated to *Agni*, the fire god. He is the presiding deity of yajna. Without fire, the yajna of civilization cannot move ahead. Imagine if there were no fire today. Civilization as it exists would crumble into pieces. I am not talking of the agni tattwa of metaphysicians. I am talking of the fire that is manifest, which is an absolute reality, with which you cook your food.

Fire is the forerunner of the entire civilization. After fire came grain. Fire and grain – this is what yajna is.

Yajna is the celebration of mankind. It is not a celebration of Hindus, Muslims or Christians, blacks or whites. We are celebrating the day when man discovered fire and grain. We light the fire by churning the *arani* (a wooden rod), and then offer grains into it. It is the celebration of the birth of civilization. When man discovered fire, he realized he could cook meat, grains, anything at all, that he could even dispose of his own body in fire and purify it. This is what yajna is all about.

The Parsees, Zoroastrians, have the tradition of fire even today. They worship the fire. However, no one except a Zoroastrian is allowed to enter a Zoroastrian temple.

SITA

The marriage of Rama and Sita took place on the fifth day of the bright fortnight of Agrahan, which is today. Tradition has it that the marriage took place at dusk. We call this hour godhuli or devadhuli. *Godhuli* means dust of cows. When the cows return home at dusk, they raise dust with their hooves, so that time is known as godhuli in India. That was the hour of Sita's wedding.

Sita was born in the north of Bihar at a place called Mithila. The people of Mithila are known as Maithils. It is a dynamic, intellectual and traditionalist society. They have now spread all over India; you will find them in the central government and parliament holding high posts.

Sita's father was Janaka, so she is also called *Janaki*, daughter of Janaka. Janaka was a great jnani. He was a *videhamukta* (one who is free of the body even while living in the body). He was not an ordinary king. If you want to know more about Janaka, you should read the *Brihadaranayaka Upanishad*. However, Sita was not really Janaka's daughter. A great famine had ravaged Mithila. There had been no rain for years. So the people of Mithila came to Janaka, the ruler, and said, "The famine cannot be averted unless you plough the land." This is the tradition in India, when the king becomes a farmer, there is no famine. When the king remains only a ruler, famines take place because he is busy looking after industries and corporate houses, not agriculturists. This is what is happening now. Guru Nanak chose to become a farmer at the fag end of his life. So when a guru or king becomes a farmer, when a king ploughs the land, there can be no famine. Therefore, the people of Mithila asked Janaka to intervene. Janaka came to till the land. There in the farmlands he found a small, new-born baby. That was Sita.

What does the word Sita mean? Have you ever seen a plough? There is a slit in it – that is called *Sita*. And *Rama* means the indweller. Just as air, moisture and light are everywhere, so Rama dwells in all hearts. Sita is the one who

91

can pierce the land, she can remove the hard core of the ego of man. After all, this is the field, the hard land full of ego, full of maya. Nobody can change you unless you have a strong Sita element in your life as well as the element of Rama. That is the meaning of 'Sita-Rama'.

Sita was a miraculous child right from birth. Janaka's family had a very big bow, which belonged to Lord Shiva. One day Janaka saw that this bow, which even the strongest of men could not move, was picked up effortlessly by Sita. He came to the conclusion that she was no ordinary girl and should be married to a person who could string the same bow. When she grew up, a *swayamvara* (marriage ceremony in which the bride chooses her husband among a gathering of men) was held, stringing the bow being the condition for marrying her. Nobody could do it, all the kings failed. Finally, it was Rama who strung the bow. So, on this day, the fifth day of Marga Shirsha, during *godhuli vela*, when the cows were returning home, she was married to Rama.

The wedding day of Sita is called *Vivaha Panchami* in North India and *Sita Kalyanam* in South India. This event did not take place five or six thousand years ago, but in Treta yuga, which goes back millions of years. Hindus have a different calculation of time. We don't believe that creation was created five thousand years ago. We believe that creation came into being billions of years ago, and mankind was born more than a billion years ago. This is also endorsed by modern science. Hindus believe that creation has a cycle of four yugas: Satya, Treta, Dwapara and Kali. The approximate age of Kali yuga is 432,000 years. Out of these, five thousand-plus years have gone by and the rest remain. We have seen the initial period of *Kali yuga*. Twice this is *Dwapara yuga*, 864,000 years, twice that is *Treta yuga* and twice that is *Satya yuga*. This is one cycle of *chatur* (four) yuga. That is the Hindu concept of time.

Sita and Rama are not mere symbols. They are part of the history of India. History has a purpose because Nature, Prakriti, always has a purpose. Sita and Rama represent us, they represent the position of our lives. What is happening in our life? What should happen in our life? What is the relationship between the self, the mind and the ego? What is the relationship between the body and the mind? What is the relationship between the body and everything else – earth, water, fire, ether? Where do we stand? All this is depicted in the lila, *avatara katha*, the story or the legend of Rama.

Great scholars in both the East and the West have said that history is facts, and yet not quite. If history is retold exactly the way the events happened, it will promote hatred. So history has to become legend. If history is reiterated as history, it will always cause dissensions, wars and hatred. If Sri Lanka were to remember that Rama destroyed it, what would happen today? The relationship between India and Sri Lanka is no longer historical. The war is not historical; it is now legendary. Legend is not myth; legend is the next form of history. The eighteen Hindu puranas are not mythology, they are legends. *Pura* means once upon a time, *na* means knowledge. The etymological meaning of *purana* is 'knowledge of once upon a time'. Therefore, correct the way you translate mythology.

The puranas are legends, and legend is the next incarnation of history. Legend becomes folklore. Folklore is not myth, but

the third incarnation of history. The story of Rama and Sita that we hear today is folklore. The songs that we sing such as *Sita Rama manohara jori, Dasharatha nandana Janaka dulari* are folksongs. History becomes legend, legend becomes folklore and folklore lives and re-lives. You can destroy history, but not folklore. Therefore, it is important that we celebrate the event of Sita and Rama's wedding. We are celebrating history, and history must be celebrated in a way that provides inspiration, enlightenment and inner awareness.

Mere remembrance of Sita-Rama takes us from outside to inside. When we say Sita-Rama, we attune with ourselves. Otherwise, we are always in tune with the external world, always extroverted. When you say Sita-Rama, Radhe-Shyam or Gauri-Shankar, the purpose is the same, to bring you back to your own consciousness, to your own self. The purpose is to be happy. They represent Prakriti and Purusha, matter and spirit, electrical wires and electricity, minus and plus. In the *Bhagavad Gita* (13:19), it is said:

Prakritim purusham chaiva viddhyaanaadi ubhaavapi
Vikaaraamshcha gunaamshchaiva viddhi prakritisambhavaan.

Know both prakriti and purusha as beginningless or eternal. Know also that all the modifications and qualities are born of prakriti.

Prakriti and Purusha are the two eternal principles of this creation. They are the principle of the universe that you see and the universe that you do not see, the imperceptible universe. Therefore, Sita without Rama, Krishna without Radha, or Shiva without Gauri is not the reality. That cannot be the reality. Reality always lies in duality, because if there is no duality, there cannot be any trinity. If there is no trinity, there is no permutation and combination, and if there is no permutation and combination, then what is all this about? This creation is an outcome of the permutation and combination of the elements of Prakriti and Purusha. Whether you talk in mathematical, metaphysical or scientific terms, it is the same. Whether you talk about unified field theory, quantum physics, Adwaita Vedanta or Dwaita Vedanta, we have to accept that there is duality with a possibility of trinity, and permutation and combination. Therein lie infinite possibilities of creation.

HEAT AND COLD

When you come to Rikhia, forget about fans, coolers and hot water. There is a story behind this. I come from Kumaon, a region in the northern hills of India. We don't know what heat is. So during the summer in Munger, by ten in the morning I would feel like a fish out of water. It was so difficult for me to survive in the heat of Munger. I used to sleep in the day and do all my work, editing, writing, etc. at night. Ultimately, we fixed an AC there. Heat was my greatest weakness, which I carried with me for a very long time. I always preferred to go to Gangotri, Badrinath or Rishikesh, not the hot plains.

When I came to Rikhia, the first thing I decided to do was to face the heat. So I did *Panchagni tapasya*. For six months, from 14th January to 16th July, from *Makar Sankranti* to *Karka Sankranti*, I would sit surrounded by four fires in four directions, the fifth fire being the sun. From morning till evening I faced the heat for nine years. I faced the heat of ninety degrees Celsius. Then I became heatproof. I am a heatproof man. I can sit under the sun like a farmer for the whole day. I do not have any problem with heat or cold, because of the five fires. *Panchagni* means five fires. There are five fires: *kama* (lust), *krodha* (anger), *lobha* (greed), *mada* (arrogance) and *moha* (delusion). That is the panchagni of the jiva. So far I have been talking about the panchagni of the body. The five fires torment the jiva; the jiva is not able to face these passions.

On 16th July I used to close down the panchagni tapasya because then it is of no use. The temperature falls after Karka Sankranti. Panchagni has to be performed when the heat is rising. So at this time I used to do *purashcharana*, repeating the guru mantra for a specified number of times. I did purash-charana one crore and eight lakh (10,800,000) times.

MANDATE

I received three instructions from my guru, Swami Sivananda: serve, love, give. These precepts became the sadhana to be perfected in my life, and took a definite form when I came to Rikhia. To help others grow and become better in all respects, external and internal, social and personal, is my sankalpa. Whatever methods I have adopted over the years, whether yoga or the activities in Rikhia, were only a means to fulfil this sankalpa. All of you must learn to live for others apart from making individual resolutions.

The Rikhia ashram will now be known as Rikhiapeeth. *Peeth* means 'seat', an apt term for Rikhia as the instructions given by Swami Sivananda have culminated and fructified here. Rikhia is an ashram in the original sense of the word, because here a lifestyle is lived. Swami Satyasangananda is the first *peethadhishwari*, or acharya, of Rikhiapeeth and has been given the sankalpa that the three cardinal teachings of Swami Sivananda will be practised and lived here. This is the future vision for Rikhia.

RIKHIAPEETH

The place where you are is called Rikhiapeeth. Just as you have Govardhan Peeth or Sharada Peeth, this is a different peeth called Rikhiapeeth. Its mantra is *Aim Hreem Kleem*. It has just been born. It is not even registered, just the naming ceremony has taken place. We will have it constitutionalized, we will have a memorandum, an association, and make it acceptable to the country and people. It will not be a Hinduistic institution. It will have a spiritual tone, not a secular tone. I do not think that secularity is right for anyone, but people say they believe in it without thinking about what it means. Nobody is secular. So Rikhiapeeth will have a spiritual tone, and at the centre of its spiritual tone will be the masses.

The salt of the earth are the poor people. Eighty percent of India is poor. They make up eighty percent of Rikhia panchayat too. It is these people we have to keep in mind. They live a pathetic life, and we have to do something to raise their standard of living. What is written in your newspapers and books is rubbish. Unless you are able to bring happiness to each and every person, your philosophy is a farce. It is meaningless. Your religions are futile.

The responsibility of religion is to help mankind, but it has never done that. Just read history. Religions have failed in this and history bears witness. The greatest wars were created by religions. The worst genocides were caused by religions. So what should be your approach to religion? At this point of time we have to see whether to re-establish religion, reconstruct religion, or reject it. We are thinking individuals. If there is a cobra in our house, how will we deal with it? We cannot say, "It is my mother's pet." Religions have to come to man's rescue, and not create more problems. Peace, *shanti*, and non-violence, *ahimsa*, should be the slogan, aim and purpose of religion. This is the religion we are talking about in the mantra *Aim Hreem Kleem*.